Information and Knowledge-based Systems
An Introduction

Information and Knowledge-based Systems
An Introduction

Ronald G. Anderson

Scott Raeburn
Lesley Beddie

Prentice Hall

New York London Toronto Sydney Tokyo Singapore

First published 1992 by
Prentice Hall International (UK) Ltd
Campus 400, Maylands Avenue
Hemel Hempstead
Hertfordshire, HP2 7EZ
A division of
Simon & Schuster International Group

Printed and bound in Great Britain by
Hartnolls Ltd, Bodmin

Library of Congress Cataloging-in-Publication Data

have been applied for

British Library Cataloguing in Publication Data

A catalogue record for this book is available from
the British Library

ISBN 0-13-457334-X (pbk)

1 2 3 4 5 96 95 94 93 92

*This book is dedicated
to the memory of
Ronald G. Anderson*

The Publisher would like to thank Sandra Anderson for her continued support and Lesley Beddie and Scott Raeburn for their valued contribution.

Contents

Preface

Efficient business operations are largely dependent upon effective information obtained from information systems or knowledge-based systems which enable executives to do the right things at the right time. This means that they are able to make decisions on the basis of facts in pursuit of objectives, rather than hunches, so removing some of the inherent risk from business ventures. This book provides a business view of such systems, explaining their purpose, advantages and disadvantages, and giving an insight into the techniques and tools used in their development. The book also makes a distinction between data, information and knowledge and between information and knowledge-based systems.

Systems can be large or small, straightforward or complex in business, and the same is true of their computer-based counterparts. The various forms of information system are described in more detail, concentrating on the business users' role in system development and the hardware and software used in information systems. The nature and importance of Executive Information Systems (EIS) in providing executives with key facts relating to business operations are also studied.

The background to how systems are created is given through a look at the stages of the software or system life cycle, from feasibility study through to full system implementation on the computer and its subsequent evaluation. The development and modelling of information systems is demonstrated using structured diagramming techniques including data flow diagrams, entity-relationship diagrams and entity life history charts. In the data processing world, few systems these days are developed without the use of CASE (Computer Aided Systems Engineering) and other software tools, so an overview of some of the relevant software is presented, covering 4GLs, CASE, application generators and query languages. Database systems are sufficiently popular and large to occupy a chapter of their own, since they usually encompass development tools and implementation tools. The chapter concludes with a look ahead into the next generation of development methods and tools – the object-oriented approach.

The primary concepts of knowledge-based systems are then introduced, encompassing knowledge representation, inferencing and reasoning – those very concepts which make them stand apart from the traditional information systems. The book concludes with some practical examples of knowledge-based systems.

Throughout the text, theory and practical aspects are intermingled, providing the business user with a knowledge and understanding of the way in which computer systems can be used to advantage in an organisation. Each chapter concludes with comprehensive revision notes with an in-built glossary of terms in context. In addition, a number of self-test questions are given and a list of texts for further reading.

The book will be found useful by students on information-oriented courses, including those provided by B/TEC, SCOTVEC, The Institute of Management Services, the Institute of Administrative Management, the Association of Accounting Technicians, the Institute of Chartered Secretaries and Administrators, City and Guilds courses, and the Chartered Institute of Finance and Accountancy.

Finally, this book has been completed by us as its original sole author died before he completed the manuscript. Of necessity the delay this caused has led to the need for revisions in the text to take account of changes in the marketplace since December 1990. Where we have had to add text, some has been adapted from our own book *An introduction to computer integrated business* and some developed from notes left by R. G. Anderson. We hope that this book will be a suitable memorial for R. G. Anderson, who introduced many to the subject of business computing over a long career.

S. Raeburn
L. A. Beddie   August 1992

Chapter 1

Management, organisation and information

INTRODUCTION AND SUMMARY

This chapter is about business, i.e any organisation which provides goods and/or services, whether profit making or not, whether private or public. It is important to appreciate that a business has a management and organisation structure consisting of relationships, responsibilities and authorities through which the business performs its activities in pursuit of defined objectives. The business structure also forms the basis of the formal communication network through which information generated by various information systems flows from one function to another. Before developing information systems it is necessary to conduct organisation and communication analysis to establish the formal structure of management and relationships, particularly those affecting more than one function, and the information flowing between them. In this context, a function refers to a part of a business with specific tasks to carry out. A function may be spread out over several locations, each doing the same type of activity. Many interfunctional relationships, particularly those emanating from the use of common data, lead to the development of integrated information systems (see Chapter 3) or databases to serve interfunctional needs. Due to these factors, this chapter provides an outline of business management and how functions may be structured in various circumstances as a preliminary to discussing their information needs. It is essential to be aware of the overall structure of a business because this provides a framework on which to build information systems for enterprise-wide requirements.

1.1 BUSINESS MANAGEMENT

Business management is almost always structured on a hierarchical basis, except in the smallest of companies. The structure of management can be depicted by an organisation chart (see Figure 1.1). The structure takes the shape of a pyramid with top management at the apex and supervisory management at the

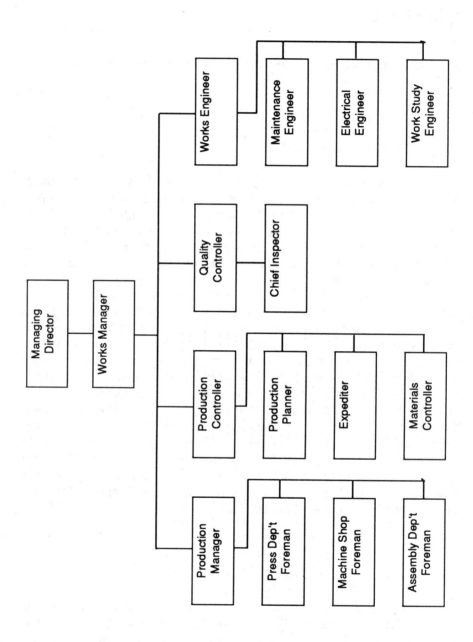

Figure 1.1 Organisation chart for manufacturing firm

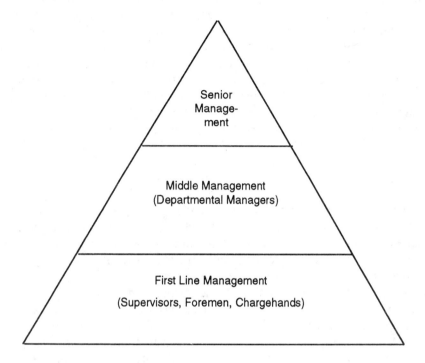

Figure 1.2 Levels of management

base (see Figure 1.2). The reason for this is the so-called span of control, i.e. a manager in each successive managerial level controls several direct subordinates, causing the structure to become progressively wider through the different tiers. Different organisations tend to have different spans of control; there is no ideal value to which a business must adhere, although similar businesses tend to be organised with similar hierarchies. A small span gives a narrow organisation, a large span a wide one.

1.1.1 Top management

The term *top management* is used to describe the board of directors in a limited company or equivalent group in other organisations. This group forms the management team responsible for formulating and executing business policy. Decisions are made at top management meetings after policy matters have been discussed. In a limited company, directors may be executive or non-executive. Non-executive directors do not play an active part in managing a business but may contribute to the formulation of policy. On the other hand, executive directors are responsible for implementing policy and for the management of a major function such as personnel, finance, production, marketing, sales, research and development, etc. The chief executive officer (usually given the title of managing director in the UK) is responsible for coordinating business operations through the other directors and functional managers. The board of directors is collectively responsible to the shareholders, the legal owners of the company.

1.1.2 Senior management

As indicated above, functions can be controlled by a director, especially in a large business. A smaller business is likely to have functional managers in charge of primary business functions reporting to the managing director. The structure of functions is discussed later in the text. A manager in charge of a function such as production in which people are controlled is called a *line manager*. Line managers are assisted in the performance of their responsibilities by various specialists in *staff functions* such as research and development. Staff functions enable line managers to concentrate on their main task, usually the production of goods and services. It is important to realise that line managers have executive authority over personnel under them in the organisation chart, but that staff managers have no executive authority outwith their own specialist function.

1.1.3 Middle management

This level of management is so described because it is positioned between senior management and supervisory management. Middle managers are often in charge of a department or section and are responsible to their respective functional manager or director. In a large business a middle manager is responsible for the running of a department within a specific functional activity. In a smaller business, a middle manager may control several functions.

1.1.4 First line management

This level of management is concerned with the direct supervision of the specialist workforce in a section of a department performing a specific task. Supervisory managers report to their respective departmental managers. A senior supervisor or foreman may deputise for the departmental manager in his or her absence. In a large organisation specialist sections may be organised in groups or teams, each led by a group or team leader, giving a lower level of supervisory management.

1.2 BUSINESS ORGANISATION

Businesses are often organised by function based on the principle of the division of labour. This specialisation facilitates training, work allocation and job scheduling, as well as more effective control. The primary activities of a large business are structured as individual functions staffed by specialists. Functions are often structured separately due to the fact that no one person can effectively control diverse, complex, large scale activities. A small business, on the other hand, is likely to combine several activities because complexity is reduced. This is attributable to the lower levels of activity in each function, which in turn is likely to generate fewer errors or less variety in the nature of problems. For example, fewer invoices may generate errors with less variety.

1.2.1 Functionalisation in a small business

A small business is likely to group several related functions together to simplify their administration and to achieve cost efficiency. This is made possible in many instances because the volume of work is less than that of a larger business. Office administration may be the responsibility of an office manager looking after a number of functions including personnel administration dealing with hiring of staff, terminations, wage and salary reviews, administration of pension schemes and office service functions typically consisting of typing, word processing, telephone, telex and fax, general postal services and reprographics. Accounting activities relating to payroll processing and the purchase, sales and general ledgers would be controlled by an accountant. Manufacturing, production, planning, stock control and purchasing functions would probably be controlled by a factory manager and marketing and sales functions including sales promotion, selling, warehouse and distribution and after-sales service by a marketing manager.

The manner in which functions are structured depends on a number of factors including the nature of the business, the skill and knowledge of management and staff as well as the cost effectiveness of a specific structure. A skilful manager would be capable of effectively administering several functions whereas a less skilled manager would not. The same considerations apply to staff because the more skilled and knowledgeable they are of various functional activities the more the grouping of functions is facilitated. Separately structured functions require a high degree of coordination and cooperation to attain corporate needs rather than fragmented functional needs. This only leads to less than optimum results for the business as a whole.

1.2.2 Functionalisation in a large business

A large manufacturing business will have a larger workload because the volume of orders from customers will probably be greater and generate a large number of manufacturing orders, despatch notes, invoices, stock transactions and ledger posting activities. In addition, a large business has more employees, creating a larger volume of work in the wages and salaries department regarding payroll processing. It is these factors which need to be considered when organising the various functions. The larger business may structure the functions separately into major areas dealing with manufacturing, marketing and sales, purchasing, accounting, personnel and stock control, etc.

1.2.3 Information and reporting systems

Functional specialists, i.e. functional managers, have the responsibility to inform line managers of all matters relating to their function. This may be concerned with financial and costing matters relating to overspending on the budget or the cost of production being too high; matters relating to the recruitment of personnel; delays in receiving essential supplies; stock shortages; production delays; quality control matters relating to the incidence of scrapped production and so on. All of these matters hinge upon the effectiveness of the information and reporting systems. Very often the information produced by one function is used by a related function and it is necessary to be aware of this, otherwise the optimisation of one function's objectives may be achieved to the detriment of those of a related function leading to the sub-optimisation of corporate achievements. This may occur, for instance, when the copy of a despatch note is not sent directly to the invoicing function which (unless the system is directly integrated) will mean that the goods despatched will not be charged to the customer. At least that would be the position initially until the oversight was noted during auditing activities perhaps. The way in which functions operate provides a framework for the development of information systems which must serve functional needs in the most effective way. This means that highly integrated functions lend themselves to the need for integrated information systems. A case in point is the integrative modularity of accounting software covering various business functional activities including payroll, invoicing, purchase, sales and general ledger and stock control.

1.3 INFORMATION AND THE LEVEL OF MANAGEMENT

1.3.1 Information needs of top management

In general executive directors in overall command of functional activities need information broad in scope but which pinpoints key factors indicating the status of the business in respect of a particular function. Executive information systems are useful for this purpose. (See Chapter 3.) On the other hand the managing director needs facts indicating the economic and financial health of the business as a whole. The exact nature of the information depends on the responsibilities of individual executives but typically includes details of current profits or profit projections compared with forecasts and with previous periods. This provides an appreciation of current trends as a basis for making decisions of action to remedy undesirable situations. For example, a lower than expected market penetration of a new product or a reduction in the sales of an established product may instigate an advertising campaign.

The trend of cash flows is important as it indicates the capability of the business to meet its commitments or otherwise assists in determining the extent 'lines of credit' require to be drawn upon and whether the situation indicates a

---

a.   Profit comparisons and trends analysed by product.
b.   Return on capital employed.
c.   Sales trends analysed by product and region.
d.   Projected cash flow forecasts.
e.   Current ratio – the total of current assets related to current liabilities.
f.   Liquidity ratio – the acid test. Relationship of liquid or near liquid current assets to current liabilities. The assets include debtors, cash at bank and cash in hand.
g.   Price/earnings ratio. This ratio indicates the relationship of the market value of the shares to earnings (profit).
h.   Status of the order book.
i.   Stage of current projects.
j.   Value of work in progress.
k.   Extent of competition.
l.   Factors providing a competitive advantage.
m.   Effectiveness of new information technology.
n.   Available lines of credit.

Box 1.1 Top management information needs

need for short-term finance, by way of overdraft facilities, or whether a share flotation is more appropriate for long-term growth and development.

Current share prices are also of great concern as they reflect the financial standing of the business which has a bearing on future share flotation and the value of the business on a 'going-concern basis'. Share prices also provide an indicator of possible take-over overtures.

1.3.2 Information needs of functional management

Functions often consist of several departments each performing specific functional activities. The marketing function may have departments for advertising and sales promotion, market research, sales and sales invoicing; warehousing and distribution; and after-sales service. Departmental managers are accountable to their functional manager who requires information summarising the activities of the various departments to enable problems to be identified with specific operational areas. The information must be sufficiently detailed to enable corrective measures to be taken to eliminate adverse situations. To this end information is required reflecting the status of current operations without unnecessary delay.

Specific information requirements depend on the nature of the function but

---

Summary of information for the marketing and sales function

a. Analysis of actual operational expenditure incurred by each department or section compared with budget.
b. Analysis of actual number of personnel employed in each department of section compared with budget.
c. Distribution costs compared with budget.
d. Warehouse costs compared with budget.

Summary of marketing and sales product information

a. Number of units sold of each product compared with target.
b. Analysis of sales value by product, customer, area and sales representative.
c. Product profitability.
d. Cost of replacing faulty products.
e. Cost of advertising analysed by product.
f. Trend of sales analysed by product.
g. Status of product life cycles.
h. Competitive information relating to specific products.

Box 1.2 Information needs for sales and marketing

Summary of information relating to sales accounting

a.   Customer account balance.
b.   Age analysis of customer account balance.
c.   Credit period agreed for each customer.
d.   Credit period allowed to each customer.
e.   Discount code for each customer.
f.   Unallocated cash from customer remittances.
g.   Total value of debtors for entry on the balance sheet.
h.   Debtor control ratio – the number of days' or weeks' sales represented by debtors.
i.   Bad debts to be written off.
j.   VAT details.

Box 1.3 Information needs for sales accounting

typically include information relating to the operational performance of each department indicating the level of operating costs incurred compared with budgets and the difference between them expressed as variances; the number of personnel employed on the various activities compared with budget; available capacity of the various activities compared with budget; available capacity of the various machines or computers in use; the amount of capital expenditure incurred on new projects including the development of new information systems and the level of productivity attained. Much of this type of information is generated by budgetary control systems. The marketing function would need information on the amount of advertising expenditure incurred and its affect on the volume of sales as well as the costs incurred on distribution and warehousing. The sales department requires the value of sales for each period analysed by customer, sales area, product group and representative compared with forecasts, etc. In addition to the information generated by budgetary control systems, functions concerned with controlling stocks and with accounting for purchases and sales require information relating to these activities.

1.3.3 Information needs of departmental management

This level of management requires detailed information which, in respect of a marketing or sales department, includes details of specific operational activities such as the value of orders received from, or cancelled by, specific customers; the level of sales revenue achieved by area, product and representative; and representatives failing to achieve sales targets, etc. It is also necessary to know the stock position of each item in the warehouse to avoid being out of stock on the one hand and overstocking on the other. In the same context credit control

Summary of operational information for the manufacturing function

a.   Analysis of actual overhead expenditure incurred by department.
b.   Analysis of budgeted overhead expenditure by department.
c.   Analysis of overhead variances by department.
d.   Analysis of actual number of personnel employed by department.
e.   Analysis of budgeted number of personnel by department.
f.   Difference in number of personnel employed and budgeted by department.
g.   Direct labour efficiency ratio by department.
h.   Idle time ratio by department.
i.   Productivity ratio by department.
j.   Quality ratio by department.
k.   Plant utilisation ratio by department.

Summary of product information for the manufacturing function

a.   Number of units produced of each product compared with target.
b.   Actual cost of direct material, direct labour and variable overheads analysed by product.
c.   Standard cost of direct material, direct labour and variable overheads analysed by product.
d.   Variances between actual and standard costs analysed by product.
e.   Number and cost of rejects analysed by product.
f.   Cost of rectification analysed by product.

Box 1.4 Manufacturing management information needs

can only be effective by being aware of the accounts status of individual customers. It is also necessary to know the number of personnel employed on various activities with the budgeted establishment and the trend in activity levels, etc.

Detailed information is necessary in all instances to be able to pinpoint situations or personnel that necessitate managerial action, to know about the achievements or efficiency of individuals and the amount of specific items of cost. Only in this way can positive action be taken because it is not possible on a global basis.

1.4 INFORMATION FOR PLANNING AND CONTROL

Planning is an essential business activity because it provides a framework, or plan, for guiding a business in the achievement of its goals and objectives. Without a plan there can be no clearly defined goals and objectives. Without a

The specific information requirements of a departmental manager depend upon the nature of the activity but the details listed below will serve to provide the general idea of typical information requirements for the effective control of activities.

a.   Employees absent analysed by reason and number of days.
b.   Machines due for maintenance.
c.   Machines out of commission analysed by reason and length of time.
d.   Employees below standard performance.
e.   Delays in work activity analysed by reason and duration.
f.   Materials in short supply.
g.   Skill shortages.
h.   Vacancies for specified jobs.

Box 1.5 Information needs of departmental managers

plan it is not possible to measure the magnitude of variations from planned results caused by random influences. Without a plan a business will tend to follow a haphazard course and implement short-term solutions to what in reality are long-term problems. What appear to be short-term deviations from the normal course of events can have long-term effects on the health and financial standing of a business. This may occur when there is a reduction in the sales of a formerly profitable product. A short-term measure to rectify the situation may be to modify the product and/or launch an intensive advertising campaign. What is really required is perhaps a new product based on current technology to attain a competitive advantage.

It is therefore essential that information systems not only provide details of normal business operations as previously discussed but must also provide information for business planning. There are basically three planning levels in a business, namely strategic, tactical and operational planning. (See Figure 1.2.)

1.4.1 Strategic planning

Strategic planning is concerned with how a company proposes to achieve its objectives. The establishment of a suitable strategy is dependent upon the availability of information relating to the company's strengths and weaknesses so that future plans can be built on its strengths while minimising the effect of its weaknesses.

When preparing strategic plans it is usual to find that potential achievements fall short of required objectives for a number of reasons. The difference between what is possible and that which is required is known as the *strategic gap*. The magnitude of the gap may be expressed in terms of a shortfall

a. Details for assessing the risks and constraints to specific courses of action.
b. Information relating to potential market opportunities for new products.
c. Information relating to potential market opportunities for existing products.
d. Facts specifying the regions qualifying for development grants.
e. Statistics portraying trends in building costs in relation to prospective building projects for new factories or offices.
f. Details of technological developments.
g. Statistics for assessing main competitors, e.g. market share.
h. Statistics specifying market trends.
i. Facts relating to economic trends, particularly the rate of inflation and interest rates.
j. The extent to which imports are restricted in specific overseas countries because of nationalistic tendencies.
k. Intelligence in respect of political issues between countries (one need only consider the Iraqi situation during 1990).
l. If operating in foreign countries it is necessary to obtain information relating to the relevant taxation laws regarding the remittance of dividends to UK shareholders.
m. Circumstances may warrant establishing information relating to the cost of producing goods in overseas countries, such as Asia, to determine whether it is more economical to supply goods to overseas markets from overseas-based factories rather than producing and supplying them from home factories.
n. Details indicating the availability of the requisite skills for the nature of the processes undertaken.

Box 1.6 Information for strategic planning

in the share of the market of a defined amount which will create a reduction in the operating profit and a lower rate of return on the capital employed. The strategic gap may be addressed to one or several constraints preventing the attainment of required objectives. The constraints may be due to a shortage of plant capacity, inadequate availability of raw materials or shortages of skilled labour. The gap may only be reduced or eliminated completely by appropriate strategies, perhaps to introduce new products before the end of the current life cycle or to break into new markets.

When preparing plans it is necessary to allow for anticipated increases in production capacity from the installation of additional plant previously commissioned and which comes into use during the planning period. Such increases in plant capacity will, it is assumed, generate additional sales revenue and profits reducing the size of the strategic gap from what it would otherwise be. If a sales promotion campaign has been undertaken then the benefits of this may arise in the current planning period and should be taken into consideration. Information is also required on product life cycles so that plans can be made to replace products at the most opportune time in order to maintain or increase profits and overall profitability. The degree of competition also requires to be assessed so that suitable counter-offensive measures may be implemented.

In conclusion, as businesses do not function as closed systems but interact with their environment, information is essential relating to developments in the economic, technological, financial, sociological and legislative spheres so that strategy can be formulated within the framework of company policies which take these factors into account.

1.4.2 Tactical planning

Tactical planning is concerned with the preparation of detailed plans to achieve strategic objectives. Information for tactical planning is obtained from an analysis of strategic plans, expanding them into greater depths of detail in respect of the factors outlined. Such plans establish the tactics to be employed in pursuit of strategic objectives. They are prepared by functional managers responsible for defined objectives as a means of achieving the overall objectives of the business. This level of planning deals with a multifarious range of factors concerned with operating a business. The factors include the planning of an effective organisation structure to achieve the corporate objectives; product market development to ensure that specified products are available in specified quantities to attain the desired level of market penetration; resource development regarding arrangements for short- and long-term finance; planning and the number of personnel required for various tasks and operations.

---

a. Details of activity levels on which to base staffing levels to attain an effective organisation structure and to assist the assessment of other resource requirements.
b. Market research information on which to base product market development plans.
c. Details for determining policy regarding the distribution of products in the various markets requiring costs and the relative effectiveness of own transport compared with leasing or hiring transport facilities whether air, road or rail.
d. Up-to-date information of technological trends to establish if certain products need updating.
e. Financial status of the business. See Box 1.1.
f. Assessment of current information systems and their suitability for future activities.

Box 1.7 Information for tactical planning

1.4.3 Operational planning

Operational planning expands the tactical plans into specific detailed plans for staffing the various functional activities and determining the number and type of machine required for the planned activities. Planning in respect of the production function commences with the previously established production quantities determined during strategic planning. It takes into account the previous years' sales volume of each product which may be used as a basis for determining future targets adjusted by a factor to reflect current sales trends in conjunction with the analysis of the order book. This will establish the quantities to manufacture of each product. This information is input to the material planning stage.

Materials planning

This element of the planning process establishes the quantity of the different component parts list of the various products. It is then necessary to determine which parts are to be bought out and which will be manufactured internally. It is then possible to establish production schedules for parts to be manufactured and purchasing schedules for parts to be bought out. These figures are adjusted by current and future stock requirements and scrap rates. The raw material requirements are established from the schedule of items to be produced internally together with a bill of materials stating the material requirement for each part.

Production planning

This element of the planning process is concerned with ensuring that the

---

a.	Quantities of each product to be manufactured by time period.
b.	Parts list of each product.
c.	Information of parts to be manufactured internally and those to be bought from external suppliers.
d.	Bill of materials for establishing material requirements for items manufactured internally.
e.	Standard times for operations.
f.	Current and proposed stock levels.
g.	Details of manning levels.
h.	Details of machine capacity.
i.	Process layouts.
j.	Scrap rates.

Box 1.8 Information for operational planning

necessary resources – labour, materials and machines – are available at the needed time to produce the required goods. A schedule listing the quantity of each product to be manufactured in a time period is used in conjunction with predetermined (or estimated) standard hours or minutes to perform each operation or process. These factors enable total hours to be computed for the parts to be manufactured during each time period. From this detail, manning levels for each process are established. The next consideration is to assess machine capacity requirements based on operation times for the parts scheduled to be manufactured. This indicates any spare or shortages of capacity enabling appropriate action to be taken to suit the circumstances. Detailed plans are then prepared allocating tasks to the various departments and sections and the determination of machine loading schedules.

1.4.4 Control information

Control information emanates from well structured, standard, routine information systems including quality, budgetary, cost, credit, stack and production control systems. All these systems incorporate the technique of management by exception as they function on the basis of variances, i.e. deviations from a specified target or standard of performance. This subject is dealt with more fully in Chapter 3.

1.5 ACHIEVING OBJECTIVES WITH COMPUTER-BASED SYSTEMS

The application of computers to achieve functional or system objectives is an effective strategy in many instances because of the inherent attributes of computers already discussed. System performance is often improved by the use of computers because of their ability to detect errors, their computational power, the speed of printing information, speedy responses to on-line enquiries and a greater control of operations by error messages and prompts. The application of a computer for achieving objectives requires that they are specified in quantitative, unambiguous terms, not stated in broad terms such as 'to make a profit', 'to expand the business to make a bigger profit' or it may simply be 'to survive'. Typical quantitaive statements of objectives are as follows:

1.   Reduce the time for producing specified reports by two days.
2.   Increase cash flows by £10,000 per month.
3.   Decrease stock holding costs by 5%.

Box 1.9 lists a number of objectives and how they may be achieved.

Objective	Method of achievement
1: Improve customer relations	a. Detect incorrect addresses and product details by validation routines. b. Speed up responses to customer sales and account enquiries by implementing an on-line order-processing system.
2: Improve cash flows	a. Produce statements of account two days after the month-end instead of the current seven days. b. Reduce the level of the inventory by an effective computer-based stock control system, leading to reduced costs of financing the inventory. c. Implement cost control procedures to reduce the cost of materials and of manufacturing operations. d. Implement a budgetary control system to control and reduce overheads. e. Implement quality control procedures to reduce the cost of scrapped production.
3: Implement or improve control procedures	a. Introduce computer-based production planning, scheduling and material planning and control systems. b. Implement a computer-based budgetary control system. c. Implement a computer-based stock control system. d. Improve control of customers' credit by making credit checks by an on-line accounts enquiry system prior to accepting a new order. e. Improve control of seat and holiday bookings by implementing a computer-based real-time system.
4: Improve the information available for decision making and problem solving	a. Implement a database with on-line terminals located in executive offices. b. Obtain more timely reports through effective computer-based systems. c. Implement an executive information system. d. Use spreadsheets to generate information from corporate data through the use of *what if. . . ?* and goal-seeking facilities. e. Apply simulation and other quantitative problem-solving techniques
5: Streamline systems	a. Separate complex integrated systems into separate sub-systems b. Integrate related sub-systems to eliminate unnecessary duplication of input data.

Box 1.9 Achieving objectives

It is important to appreciate that the objectives of each individual system or function should be coordinated and not established in isolation. All such objectives are an integral element of the overall objectives of a business as a corporate entity. If the objectives of individual systems fail to be achieved then corporate objectives will not be achieved. Objectives may be structured on a hierarchical basis whereby the various functions, departments and sections, which may be defined as sub-systems, have their own sub-objectives.

Corporate objective:
      a.   Increase profit.

Functional objectives – Marketing:

      a.   Increase sales of product A by x %.
      b.   Increase profitability of product B by y %.

Departmental objectives:
      a.   Reduce delivery time of product A from 14 days to seven days to eliminate the reason for loss of orders due to delays.
      b.   Reduce the costs of manufacturing product B by improving the method of production or reduce the level of rejects by more stringent quality control.

Box 1.10 Hierarchy of objectives

When objectives are found to be impractical or unattainable then they must be redefined as it is pointless attempting to accomplish fictitious aims.

1.6 REVISION NOTES

1. A business consists of an organisation structure comprising relationships, responsibilities and authorities through which the business performs its activities in pursuit of defined objectives. An objective may be defined as a business aim, target, goal or required result.
2. An organisation structure represents the formal communication network through which information flows from one function to another. The information required by the different functions depends on the nature of their activities. An organisation structure also indicates how functions are coordinated (structured) to form working groups for achieving optimum results in the performance of specified tasks in pursuit of objectives. It also specifies superior/subordinate relationships – the command structure.
3. Before developing information systems it is necessary to conduct an

organisation and communication analysis to establish the information flowing between functions. An organisation analysis establishes the structure of a section, department, function or a complete business in respect of working groups and the respective levels of management. A communication analysis indicates interfunctional information flows which currently exist providing details of intercommunications between working groups.

4. The overall structure of a business provides a framework on which to build information systems for enterprise-wide requirements.

5. Business management is often structured on a hierarchical basis forming the shape of a pyramid. Management may be defined in a number of ways including:
    (a) The art of dealing with people.
    (b) Personnel with responsibility for achieving the efficient performance of specified business activities and the effective use of resources.
    (c) Personnel with executive authority.
    (d) Personnel who make decisions.

6. Businesses are normally organised by function based on the principle of specialisation. A function may be defined in two different ways:
    (a) In the context of a business organisation a function may be described as a specialist activity performed by a homogeneous group of personnel, the function being controlled by a functional manager.
    (b) In the context of a business application or information system a function is an alternative term to operation or task.

7. Functional specialists have the responsibility to inform line managers of all matters relating to their function.

8. Management information needs become progressively more detailed the lower the level of management. Conversely, information needs become progressively less detailed the higher the level of management.

9. Top management require key facts indicating the status of the business as a whole.

10. Planning is an essential business activity because it provides a framework for achieving its objectives.

11. Strategic planning is concerned with how a company proposes to achieve its objectives.

12. Tactical planning establishes the tactics to be employed to achieve strategic objectives.

13. Operational planning expands the tactical plans into detailed plans for the various functional activities.

14. Control information emanates from well structured, routine information systems.

15. Computers are often used to assist in the achievement of functional

objectives because of their computational and logical attributes and their ability to detect errors and process data at high speed.

1.7 SELF-TEST QUESTIONS

1. What is an organisation structure and its significance to business information needs?
2. Before developing information systems it is necessary to conduct organisation and communication analyses. State the purpose of such analyses.
3. How would you define the term 'management'?
4. What is a business function and on what basis are they organised?
5. Differentiate between strategic, tactical and operational planning.
6. Why is planning an essential business activity?

1.8 FURTHER READING

1. *Management Theory and Principles*, Tony Proctor, M. & E. Handbooks/Pitman: London, 1982. Refer to chapters III—IX.
2. *Business Data Systems*, 4th edn., H. D. Clifton, Prentice Hall International: Hemel Hempstead, 1990. Refer to chapters 1 and 2.
3. *Information Analysis*, Janice Burn and Mike O'Neil, Paradigm/Blackwell Scientific Publications: Oxford, 1987. Refer to chapter 2.
4. *Business Systems and Information Technology*, R. G. Anderson, Paradigm/Blackwell Scientific Publications: Oxford, 1988. Refer to chapters 2 and 3.
5. *A Dictionary of Management Terms*, R. G. Anderson, M. & E. Handbooks/Pitman: London, 1983. General reference.
6. *Information and Management Systems, Concepts and applications*, Mike Harry, Pitman: London, 1990. Refer to chapter 1.

Chapter 2

Data, information and knowledge-based systems

INTRODUCTION AND SUMMARY

This chapter defines the nature of data and its relationship to information as a prerequisite to a further study of systems dealt with in Chapters 3, 4 and 5. It is important to appreciate that the terms data and information are not synonyms. Data is the input element of an information processing system. This chapter also introduces the concept of knowledge-based systems prior to their detailed discussion in Chapter 10.

2.1 DATA DEFINED

Data can simply be defined as facts about a particular subject, but further explanation is necessary to enable the term to be more fully understood. Data may be classified into the two broad categories of primary and secondary.

2.1.1 Primary data

Primary data relates to many different situations and may be collected in a variety of ways. For example, data relating to the number of gallons of petrol contained in a garage storage tank is usually obtained by taking a reading from a dipstick previously inserted in the tank. A similar method is used to measure the amount of oil in the sump of a car engine. The amount of petrol in the tank of a car is read from a petrol gauge, the reading of which is generated by a sensor in the tank. The speed of an engine is measured in revolutions per minute which can be read from a tachometer. Similarly, the speed of a vehicle can be read from a speedometer and so on. From a business viewpoint data may be classed as *primary data* which relates to facts collected during the course of business activities. Such facts may be defined as processed and uncorrelated details of business transactions which are collected into homogeneous groups for transformation into information. Many business transactions originate in the form of source documents containing handwritten or printed details of transactions, examples of which are listed in Box 2.1.

Purchase order. This document informs the supplier of a customer's specific requirements. Typically the details it contains are:

a.	Order number	g.	Item or commodity code
b.	Date of order	h.	Quantity required
c.	Delivery date	i.	Price each
d.	Name		
e.	Invoice address		
f.	Delivery address		

Items g to i would be repeated for each separate commodity on the order.

Clock card. Records attendance hours of employees and typically contains the following details:

a.   Employee number (clock number)
b.   Departmental code
c.   Week ending date
d.   Hours worked normal time
e.   Hours worked premium time – 1.5 (time and a half)
f.   Hours worked premium time – 2 (double time)

Box 2.1 Examples of primary data

Despatch notes record details of despatches to customers; issue notes record details of materials and parts obtained from the stores and so on. The nature of the documents depends upon the type of business because there is obviously a difference in the nature of the transactions performed by banks – a cheque or paying-in slip; tour operators – a holiday booking form; insurance companies – an insurance proposal form; a building society – a mortgage payment or cash withdrawal form, and so on.

2.1.2 Secondary data

This type of data already exists and may consist of published statistics or internal records relating to specific subjects. As statistics and internal records soon become dated it is important to verify that they are still valid before being used. Box 2.2 shows some examples of secondary data categories.

2.1.3 Data structures

Data for processing by traditional information systems must be well defined. Data is stored in computers as a series of binary patterns, most commonly as

> a. External environment data which includes matters relating to social, political and economic factors.
> b. Competitive data which embraces details with regard to the performance of main competitors, their present activities and future plans.
> c. Internal environment data of a qualitative and quantitative type relating to quality control, levels of performance, costs, overheads, profits and losses, financial strength and weakness relating to cash flows and lines of credit.
> d. Organisational data relating to manpower levels, the structure of departments including the span of control

Box 2.2 Categories of secondary data

characters. Each character is associated with a specific binary pattern and a list of these patterns is called a code. The most well-known code for storing data in computers is probably ASCII – the American Standard Code for Information Interchange – which is universal in personal computers and minicomputers. Some large mainframe computers, from IBM and other companies, use a different code known as EBCDIC – Extended Binary Coded Decimal Information Code.

In order to store large amounts of data, characters are grouped into fields. These are combined to form records, and a collection of records form a file.

Fields

The term field is used to describe a unit of data relating to a transaction. A field may consist of alphabetic characters for descriptive needs including employee, customer and supplier names, description of expenses, stock items, locations and products, etc.; numeric fields for storing fixed and floating point numbers for computational requirements; logical fields and memo fields. Each field is identified by a field name. A field stores the value of a variable which can be different for each occurrence of a transaction. The amount of an insurance premium payable by clients, for example, will be specific to individual clients and will be recorded in the same field but on different records. Fields, also referred to as *attributes* or *data items*, need to be defined precisely by specifying the following factors:

1. name of the field;
2. length of the field in characters;
3. type of character to be stored in the field;
4. range of values for validation purposes;
5. if it is to be used for indexing;
6. if it is to be used in calculations.

Although a data item may have a variable number of characters, e.g. a person's surname, the most common type of field is one with a specified length, i.e. the maximum number of characters allowed, once defined, cannot easily be altered. This is because it is much easier to write software to cope with so-called *fixed length* fields. It is therefore important to estimate field lengths accurately before starting to store data.

Records

Related fields combine to describe the attributes of a specific type of record relating to a particular type of transaction. Examples are payroll records which store details of employees' earnings and tax; customer records containing details of credit sales to, and remittances from, customers; and supplier records containing the value of credit purchases from, and remittances to, suppliers. Each record is identified and referenced by a record key or key field. Box 2.3 provides examples of the attributes or fields relevant to typical customer and payroll records.

Customer record		Payroll record	
Field content	Field type	Field content	Field type
Account number	Character	Employee number	Character
Name	Character	Name	Character
Address	Character	Department code	Character
Credit limit	Numeric	Taxable gross pay	Numeric
Discount category	Character	(to date)	
Account balance	Numeric	Tax (to date)	Numeric
Analysis of balance	Numeric	Taxable gross	Numeric
(aged)		(previous employment)	
		Tax	Numeric
		(previous employment)	
		NI number	Character
		Employee's NI to date	Numeric
		Total NI contributions	Numeric
		(to date)	
		Holiday credit to date	Numeric
		Other deductions	Numeric

Box 2.3 Example of record structures

In most systems, each record which refers to a specific entity has to have the same fields as every other record, although some fields may have no entry, e.g. home telephone number in an employee record. Records which have a specified number of fields, each of a specified length, are known as *fixed length* records.

Files

A file consists of a homogeneous group of records relating to a specific application such as payroll, customers, suppliers, etc. Each record has a *record number* allocated by the operating system of the computer. Although a file may have a variable number of records, most files have fixed length records. This makes the software which manipulates the file easier to develop and maintain. The records in a file may be in a random, i.e. unspecified, sequence or an order may be imposed by sorting the records into a pattern to allow the easier storage and retrieval of records. The sort order is based on the contents of one or more fields, known as *keys*.

Keys

Keys facilitate the retrieval of specific records from a database and from direct access files in on-line applications. Two types of keys or *key fields* can be specified for a file. A *primary* key, normally consisting of a code number, is allocated to logical records such as the accounts of customers and suppliers, to stock items, employees, products and departments, etc. Each key value uniquely identifies a specific logical record and all fields comprising each record must be related to the primary key. Each primary key value can occur only once in a file. These matters are discussed within the topic of normalisation in Chapter 9. The primary key is also used as the sort key to arrange the records in a file in a specific sequence, often ascending alphabetic or numeric sequence. Thus the records in a transaction file are arranged to match the sequence of records on a master file. This avoids having to search a file for a specific record during file updating as they are dealt with sequentially.

A *secondary* key consists of a descriptive field such as a customer or supplier name, or a combination of two or more fields. A file may have many secondary keys, depending on the need for information retrieval. Secondary keys are not used to arrange the sequence of records, but do allow the appearance of having the records in a different sequence from the primary key. Secondary key values are also allowed to have duplicates, i.e. more than one record with the same key value. Thus a secondary key may not uniquely identify a single record. Secondary key access to a file is usually done by constructing a separate *index file* for each secondary key.

Index files

An index file contains a list of secondary key values and the corresponding record numbers or primary key values. To find a record with a specified secondary key value, e.g. a surname, the software finds the surname in the index file, reads the corresponding record number or primary key, e.g. an employee number, and then directly accesses the main file using that value. This is much faster than searching the entire file looking for the surname. This use of an index is analogous to the use of an index in a library to find a specific book when, say, only the title or subject is known.

Note that many file handling packages for personal computers use index files for all keys and therefore do not have a primary key as such. The manuals will only talk about how to build indexes, not the different types of keys available.

2.1.4 Data capture methods

The primary objective of data capture methods is to collect data in the most efficient and economical way, avoiding where possible the need to convert it from human-sensible form, i.e. normal handwritten characters on source documents, to machine-sensible form on magnetic disk. In both single- and multi-user environments the input of transaction data from source documents is usually by human operator using a terminal keyboard. This method is applied in many types of business, large and small.

In high volume environments, however, the direct entry of data by terminal keyboard may be considered to be too slow. Data may need to be encoded directly to magnetic disk to reduce the time it takes to input transaction data. This can be achieved by a variety of means, some of which are described below. All eliminate the need for a separate time-consuming and costly data conversion operation.

Point of sale (POS) systems

Supermarkets have a special need for an effective system of data capture to provide a fast throughput of customers in order to avoid lengthy queues and delays which create frustration for both staff and customers. The technique uses a laser scanning device to read details of products encoded in a bar-coded label attached to the goods. The code is referred to as EAN (European Article Number). The data captured in this way is transmitted to an in-store computer for pricing the goods purchased by customers; producing a till receipt itemising each purchase, the total amount, the value of the note given to the cashier in payment and the change which is due; stock management and the procurement of new supplies.

Banks – auto teller terminals

Banks use auto teller terminals for collecting details of cash dispensed automatically. The data collection technique adopted in this instance is by means of a special keyboard and a magnetic card reader. The keyboard allows customers to enter their personal identification number (PIN), the service required and the amount of money (if any) needed. The card reader uses the plastic card issued to the customer by the bank which contains details of their bank account and allows the PIN to be validated.

Portable computers

Many firms now use portable computers for, say, collecting stock control data in large stores or collecting sales information whilst sales representatives are visiting customers. One firm which offers a TV and video repair service has repair technicians who visit customers in their own homes. Details of the jobs to be done are sent to a hand-held computer over the telephone when the technician dials into Head Office. The main computer also gets details of the jobs completed, the time spent and the parts used from the technician's computer, which also prints receipts for customers.

Handprint data entry

Some computers have special touch-sensitive pads which can sense lines drawn with a suitable pen. The shape created can then be interpreted as an alphabetic or numeric character, converted into ASCII code and transmitted to a host computer.

Data recorders

These are used in factories and other locations which involve machinery. The data recorder is used to capture details of machine operations performed on jobs, either manually or automatically.

2.2 INFORMATION

Information reduces uncertainty and enables the most suitable action to be taken by managers and other personnel to attain system objectives. Information also enables well informed decisions to be made because it enables a greater depth of judgement to be applied to business problem areas.

Information often results from processed data, e.g. as exception reports, as a complete listing of the contents of a master file, the list of customer balances from the customer file; a list of insurance premiums due, a list of holiday bookings for specific destinations on a particular date. Box 2.4 gives some further examples of information.

(a) Accounting documents:
    Invoices
    Credit notes
    Statements of account

(b) Schedules or lists:
    List of invoices, credit notes and adjustments
    Remittance list
    Accounts list
    Stock list
    List of fixed assets – buildings and plant and machinery

(c) Management reports:
    Aged analysis of debtor (customer) balances, i.e. the amounts owing by time period
    Sales trends
    Status of the order book – the value of orders received
    Stage reached of specified contracts
    Value of work in progress

(d) Exception report:
    Stocks below minimum safety level
    Accounts exceeding allowed credit limit
    Overheads exceeding budget
    Costs exceeding standard
    Contracts likely to incur penalty payments for late completion
    Outstanding loan repayments
    Tenants with rent arrears
    Holidays available at short notice
    Outstanding insurance premiums for car or building insurance, etc.

Box 2.4 Information examples

2.2.1 Information attributes

Management need information to enable them to make well balanced decisions and to control business operations efficiently to achieve a defined objective. Thus information is usually required relating both to current situations and to past events to obtain, for example, statistical trends.

To allow management to use it effectively, information should:

- enable management to make effective decisions;
- be suitable for taking effective control action;
- be compatible with the responsibilities of specific managers;
- contain an appropriate level of detail for the needs of the recipient – not too detailed or too summarised;
- relate to the current situation;
- be reliable, i.e. of an acceptable level of accuracy;
- be timely, i.e. available in an appropriate response time;
- be based on the exception principle by disclosing variances in appropriate circumstances.

2.2.2 Timeliness of information

The importance of the delay factor, a function of the timeliness of information, is critical to the effective operation of many businesses. The delay factor is a measure of the time from when an event occurs to when information is received about the event. Recording events as they occur requires the use of a computerised information system in many instances because of its ability to deal with high volumes of transactions speedily. Such systems process events as they occur on the basis of individual transactions and because of this are referred to as transaction processing systems.

Real-time systems are dynamic, accepting random input at random time intervals, and accordingly the content of information files is changed dynamically. This means that in an airline seat reservation system the number of seats available on each flight is decreased as seats are reserved. When an enquiry is made from a travel agent the actual number of seats available is displayed on the terminal screen. This may change as the screen is observed due to seat bookings on other terminals.

The delay factor in manufacturing can be extremely critical because it can have the effect of delaying despatches which can have the effect of losing future orders. If information relating to operational delays or delays in receiving critical materials is not immediately reported then no action can be taken to remedy the situation. This can cause a considerable loss, incurring the cost of idle facilities and causing the under-absorption of fixed factory overheads.

In a factory the status of work-in-progress is updated each time an order is completed or when a new order is started thereby providing information on the actual status of a system at any moment in time. This is achieved by factory data recorders strategically located in different parts of the factory.

Less critical business activities are processed in batches. This applies to sales to customers which can be invoiced and recorded in the respective customers' account several days after the goods are despatched. These transactions are of a routine accounting nature unaffected by a critical delay factor. This does not mean to imply that invoicing and similar activities should be delayed from their normal time schedule – they should not. It does imply, however, that invoices need not be processed immediately items are despatched but this depends to some extent on the volume of transactions which may warrant processing as despatches take place to avoid backlogs.

2.2.3 Noise and redundancy

The term *noise* has a special meaning in the context of information systems. Noise in this context can be stated to mean any environmental influence distorting information or messages being passed from one location to another, or between one person and another, causing it to be received in a form different to that which was intended. When personnel are passing information to each other verbally, noise may occur as a result of a person in the vicinity shouting loudly, or due to a noisy machine, a vehicle or an aircraft passing overhead, all of which cause the person to whom the information is transmitted to receive incorrect or partial facts. Noise may also occur when requests for information contain either the wrong or inaccurate subject matter. Either way it causes disruption to the smooth operation of business activities.

Noise in telecommunications can be defined as the presence of unwanted signals in communications causing the signal received to differ from that transmitted. The presence of noise on a telephone line has the effect of distorting the information being communicated. Unless the information is retransmitted it may cause the wrong action to be taken, but even if it is retransmitted the speed of communications is reduced and time is wasted. Obviously the effect of noise must be eliminated to avoid its consequential effect on efficient communications. A remedy to eliminate the effect of noise in telecommunications is the incorporation of redundancy checking.

Redundancy is a means of ensuring that information is received correctly. In its simplest form the term is used to describe the addition of extra characters in a report to ensure it is interpreted without ambiguity and misunderstandings. For example, in a report explaining that a capital expenditure project will cost £50,000 the amount can also be spelled out for comparison with the numeric value (i.e. five thousand pounds). Without the inclusion of redundancy it could have been accepted as 5,000 when it should have been 50,000 or 50,000 when it should have been 5,000 causing cash flow problems and potential difficulties when arranging lines of credit via overdrafts or loans.

Redundancy checking in data transmission systems detects errors by comparing bit patterns in the blocks of data being transmitted. Blocks found to contain errors are then automatically retransmitted. Errors may also be detected by the technique of parity checking. Errors in communications may also be detected by retransmitting signals received back to the transmitting terminal on a separate channel. The signals are then compared with the original transmission. Differences indicate the presence of transmission errors.

2.2.4 Information systems

The data in such systems is well structured, forming sets of contiguous records stored in files. Data is retrieved from the various files to produce reports and administrative documents. Applications are programmed in procedural languages such as COBOL or PL/1 which state what to do and how to do it to within a program. They do, of course, have the capability of dealing with predefined conditions encountered during the course of running a program. Such systems are of a routine nature applying on-line or batch processing techniques. An example of procedural code using Structured English and relating to a simplified payroll application is shown in Box 2.5. This may be contrasted with the style of programming used with a database and the nature of the production rules used with an expert system for arriving at a conclusion. Payroll details of employees are stored in a master file. Current pay details are entered by keyboard. After various computations details are printed on a payroll. The printed details include the departmental number of the employee, employee clock number, wages earned and tax for the current pay period and cumulative earnings and tax to date.

```
READ payroll master record
WHILE (not end of file) DO
        REPEAT
                INPUT (hours worked and rate of pay)
                COMPUTE (wages and tax)
                SUM (wages and wages to date)
                SUM (tax and tax to date)
                PRINT (department number, employee clock number, wages  and
                tax current period, wages and tax to date)
        UNTIL (end of transactions)
        READ payroll master record
ENDWHILE
PRINT (payroll totals)
```

Box 2.5 Procedural code example

Traditional information systems produce information after subjecting transaction data to a series of operations including data validation routines to ensure the integrity of data; sorting routines to arrange transactions in sequential order to facilitate access to records stored on magnetic disks for reference and updating; computing the value of transactions, file updating to ensure records contain the current status of the particular entity, the account balance of customers and suppliers, for instance, and printing out information according to the needs of each application. Traditional information systems produce routine information for administrative and accounting purposes as shown in the list summarising examples of information.

Information often needs to be transmitted from one point in an organisation to another, for example a message may be transmitted from a terminal in one location to a terminal in another part of the business using electronic mail facilities. In other instances, information may be transmitted from a centralised computer installation to a remote terminal located at a branch factory or office. Whatever the means of communication, it is essential that information flows from its point of origination to its designated destination because only when information is received can it be acted upon. It is perhaps an important point to state that well structured information systems are required to meet the formal information needs of a business. There also exists, however, informal information flows communicated between personnel in the same or related working environment. This type of information often plays an important role in the efficient running of a business because action can be taken to modify a particular situation from a verbal statement indicating that a particular order is falling behind on its delivery date or that a wrong part has been supplied for a machine. A formal information system would probably report these facts during its normal reporting cycle but may induce unnecessary delay in dealing with the specific situations. It all depends if the reporting cycle is sufficient for its purpose. This is the reason why many information systems are of a real-time nature enabling critical situations to be communicated and dealt with as they arise.

Databases which store large volumes of structured data in tables have made the management of information more flexible and accessible by the non-computer expert compared with the traditional information processing systems. This is because of their relatively user-friendly nature, especially those with pull-down menus allowing the selection of options by pick and point techniques using a mouse or keyboard. They allow speedy access to records and fast responses to queries. Different views can also be obtained of information for varying purposes.

2.2.5 Information and change

The business environment in which individual companies operate changes dynamically due to the pressure of economic forces, competition, new legislation, changing consumer preferences, technological developments and political factors. The Single European Market, which brings changes in the European Community trading rules, is one such example. The activities of a business must respond to such random events to remain viable and accordingly systems must be modified, or retuned, to be compatible with changing circumstances. Unless this is done meaningless information will flow through the various functions causing incorrect decisions to be made which will be catastrophic to business prosperity.

Information is generated by information systems designed for existing circumstances and foreseeable future needs but even so will need to be amended for changing situations in the external environment. Due to this factor businesses often need to be reorganised so that they are more able to contend with change. This will affect the functional structure necessitating the separation of departments in some instances and the consolidation of others. This requires the inception of new information flows and changes to the systems which produce them for the new organisation to be effective. It will be appreciated without doubt that information unrelated to current circumstances serves no useful purpose and can in fact drastically affect the future profitability of the business.

2.3 KNOWLEDGE-BASED SYSTEMS

Traditional information systems process transaction data through a series of transformation operations into meaningful information. Knowledge is information in some sort of human context, based on experience or learning. Thus a *knowledge-based* system needs to hold relevant details of what is normally in the mind of a human and to interpret its output in that context. The process of putting knowledge into a suitable format for computer processing is tricky and time consuming, and special techniques have been developed to make the procedures easier.

The fundamental difference between traditional information systems and knowledge-based systems (KBS) is that KBS simulate human reasoning and judgemental capabilities. KBS are either rule and/or object based, dealing with less structured or abstract data types. Traditional information systems do not possess judgemental capabilities but process data by predefined programs written in procedural code. Knowledge-based systems are discussed in greater depth in Chapter 10.

2.3.1 Fourth generation languages and expert systems

Fourth generation languages (4GLs) were developed for mainstream data processing applications, greatly simplifying their development with non-procedural language and English-like enquiry and reporting facilities.

An *expert system* is a computerised knowledge-based system which simulates human behaviour by making deductions using the rules of logical inference. The integration of 4GLs and expert systems to form strategic information and knowledge management systems is an inevitable stage in the evolutionary development of systems.

Expert systems grew out of scientific and academic research for dedicated hardware, requiring exceptional skills in the use of specialist operating systems and languages such as LISP and Prolog. Expert systems have now moved out of the laboratory environment and away from special hardware environments such as LISP workstations having proved themselves in PC environments. Prime examples of applications which can benefit from expert systems include applications where complex rules are involved in arriving at a conclusion. It is very difficult and time consuming to code these rules using procedural or 4GL techniques and, before the advent of expert systems, there was no substitute for human expertise and judgement in this field.

Ideally the required knowledge will be *embedded* in the information system handling that part of an application requiring judgemental and reasoning capabilities. The application of judgemental procedures then becomes part of the normal sequence of processing transactions, rather than a separate operation requiring extensive human involvement. As an example, an insurance proposal for a stated risk would be validated by the traditional information systems. The knowledge system module would then be automatically invoked to pass judgement on the viability of the risk before switching back to the information systems to update the information files or a database.

Embedded knowledge systems also have great potential in the field of sales, where they can be used within 4GL-based sales order processing systems for, say, complex pricing applications. As an example, consider a firm which has delivery charges dependent on distance, the order value and customer status. The rules used state that no delivery charges are to be made for distances under five miles, delivery charges are to be made for distances over five miles IF the value of an order is less than a stated amount OR the customer's account balance is overdue, etc. This type of problem can get quite complicated, with lots of potential for mistakes. A simple expert system could use a coded version of the rules to ensure accuracy and consistency of charging.

2.4 REVISION NOTES

1. Data is both a singular and plural term which describes a single fact or a collection of facts relating to business transactions.
2. Primary data from a business viewpoint consists of facts collected during the course of business activities relating to specific transactions.
3. Data structures may consist of groups of data (fields) which store attributes (specific value of variables) relating to a particular type of business transaction which form a business record. An attribute is any detail which quantifies, qualifies or describes an entity. In other instances, particularly in a database, data may be structured in relational tables. Other forms of structure include hierarchical and network structures which are discussed in Chapter 7.
4. The characteristics of a field need to be defined by such factors as the name of the field, the number and type of characters held and the range of values for validation purposes.
5. Data types include descriptive data for names and addresses and describing stock items, etc.; numeric data for fixed and floating point numbers to be used in computations; logical data such as relational operators AND, OR, for instance; memo fields providing supporting details in relation to fields and special date fields for the manipulation of dates.
6. Records consist of combinations of related fields with regard to a particular type of transaction.
7. A primary key uniquely identifies a specific logical record and all fields comprising each record must be related to the primary key.
8. A secondary key may consist of a descriptive field such as a customer name which must be consistent with a primary key, such as a customer number, before a transaction is accepted for processing. Consistency is checked during a data validation routine.
9. Files consist of homogeneous groups of records relating to a specific application such as payroll.
10. The primary objective of data capture methods and techniques is to collect and record transaction data in the most efficient and economical way.
11. Information is not to be confused with data. Information is the product of processing data.
12. Information reduces uncertainty allowing managers to take the most suitable action to attain objectives.
13. Information often needs to be transmitted from one location to another.
14. The business environment changes dynamically and businesses must respond to such changes in order to remain economically viable. This often requires information systems to be modified to ensure they produce information compatible with the current (changed) situation.

15. The term noise has a special meaning in the context of information systems. It relates to environmental influences, rather than physical noise, which distort information causing the signals received to differ from those transmitted.

16. Redundancy also has a special meaning in the context of generating reports. The term is used to describe the addition of extra (redundant) characters in a report, e.g. the spelling of an amount in addition to its numeric value to ensure it is interpreted without ambiguity. If an anomaly arises it is checked to determine the correct value, e.g. when a numeric figure of £1,000 is accompanied by redundant characters stating an amount of ten thousand pounds. The question to ask is which is the correct amount, £1,000 or £10,000?

17. A delay factor is a function of the timeliness of information and is a critical factor in some circumstances, especially in real-time systems.

18. The cost of producing information needs to be controlled just as manufacturing costs in a factory are controlled.

19. Expert systems grew out of scientific and academic research but have now moved out of the laboratory to the real world embracing scientific, engineering and administrative applications.

20. Traditional information systems process well structured data by means of procedural languages.

21. The fundamental difference between traditional information systems and knowledge-based systems is that the latter simulate human reasoning and judgemental capabilities.

2.5 SELF-TEST QUESTIONS

1. Define the terms 'data' and 'information'.
2. State the meaning of the term 'data structures'.
3. Define and give examples of 'data types'.
4. Define and state the relationship between a primary and a secondary key.
5. What does a file consist of?
6. Why is information useful to managers?
7. Why does a business need to respond to changes in the environment?
8. What is the significance of the term 'noise' in an information sense?
9. State the meaning of the terms 'delay factor' and 'redundancy' in the context of an information system.
10. What is the fundamental difference between information and knowledge-based systems?

2.6 FURTHER READING

1. *Information Analysis*, Janice Burn and Mike O'Neil, Paradigm/Blackwell Scientific Publications: Oxford, 1987. Refer to chapter 3.
2. *Computer Studies: A first year course*, Ron Anderson, Blackwell Scientific Publications: Oxford, 1990. Refer to chapter 13.
3. *Crash Course in Artificial Intelligence and Expert Systems*, Louis E. Frenzel, Jr (SAMS), Howard W. Sams & Co.: Indianapolis, 1987. Refer to chapter 1.

Chapter 3

Information systems characteristics and structure

INTRODUCTION AND SUMMARY

This chapter commences by discussing the characteristics of information systems and how their elemental structure coincides with those of a computer system. The chapter continues by considering the concepts of a total system, the total systems approach to systems development and the nature of integrated systems. An important requirement of many information systems, particularly those of a control nature, is that they should incorporate a feedback control loop to enable management to take appropriate action based upon variances from planned or budgeted performance. This is dealt with by the inclusion of an introduction to cybernetics.

3.1 INFORMATION SYSTEMS CHARACTERISTICS

An information system is a system which collects, records, stores and computes business transactions data and presents the results of processing to appropriate personnel in an organisation in the form of information. The information is then used to assist in the effective administration of a business, for controlling business operations and as a basis for making effective decisions. Very often information systems are extensions to existing data processing systems. For example, an order processing system has the primary purpose of processing customers' orders but which can also provide valuable information for a number of requirements. Information which may be provided includes product shortages indicating the back order situation; age analysis of customers' outstanding account balance for credit control purposes; analysis of sales by area, customer, value and representative, etc., for comparison with current targets and previous years' achievements for obtaining trends. An information system must be capable of providing information about business events as and when required with an acceptable degree of accuracy. Many information systems are computerised for this purpose because they are able to process large volumes of data at high speed with a high degree of accuracy. Some may also be capable of real-time processing, i.e. handling details of events as they occur.

Some information systems are simple systems providing information relating to one specific business application such as payroll processing. Other systems consist of combinations of several smaller (sub-)systems and may be classed as complex systems, an example of which is shown in Figure 3.1.

A prerequisite of any effective information system is its ability to access information immediately regardless of where or how it is stored. A system is required which integrates different computers running on different operating systems, both internally and externally, into a single unified computing and information resource. Systems which use this approach have an *open systems architecture*.

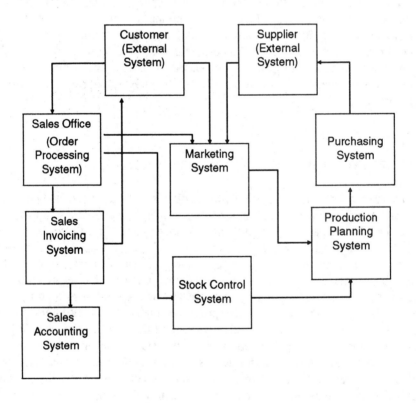

Figure 3.1 An integrated system

3.1.1 Elements of an information system

All information systems consist of four primary elements. *Inputs* consist of transaction data which the organisation has some interest in. *Processing* is the conversion of input data into a form suitable for storage and retrieval. *Storage* consists of some device (usually magnetic) for holding data for a long period. *Outputs* consist of reports and listings of the data held in storage manipulated according to specified rules. The details shown in Box 3.1 provide a composite view of a number of typical business applications.

Application	Input	Processing	Storage	Output
Order processing	Customer orders	various	Orders file	Sales analysis Back-order report
Sales accounting	Customer orders	various	Sales ledger	Aged debtors analysis
Purchase accounting	Purchase invoices	various	Purchase ledger	Purchase analysis
Payroll	Payroll data, clock cards, etc.	various	Payroll file	Wages analysis

Box 3.1 Systems view of typical business applications

The elements of an information system coincide with those of a computer system which consists of an *input device* for entering data into a *processor* where processing operations take place. Details of records required for reference or updating during processing are retrieved from a *storage device* and updated records are written back to the storage device. Current information requirements are output by an *output device.*

3.2 THE SYSTEMS APPROACH

Although the development of information systems is dealt with later in this book, it is useful at this juncture to consider the total systems approach to systems development. This approach recognises that all business systems when combined form a complete business entity.

The development of individual systems without considering how they relate to others in the organisation is known as a piecemeal approach and can cause sub-optimisation. For example, the same data being input and processed by several different systems causes duplicated data flows and processing activities. In some instances information required by a related system may not be produced causing disruption. To avoid such situations the systems approach involves a detailed analysis of all business systems in order to define the relationships between inputs, files and outputs as well as types of information required by specific managers for control and decision making.

An integrated system is representative of how an organisation is structured whereby each function is related to other functions either directly or indirectly forming a total system. Some are directly related because of the physical activities carried out, others are related by information flows. The physical activities of one function represented as data or information flows are processed by another function. This occurs when details of physical shop floor activities relating to the work of employees, for instance, are represented by clock cards which record attended time as a basis for computing wages by hours worked and job tickets which record details of work done for computing wages based on payment-by-results (PBR) schemes. These details are passed to the payroll section for preparing payslips, payrolls, credit transfers and other payroll statistics. It is more of an ideal rather than a practical reality to have a tightly integrated system which exactly mirrors the physical structure of the business. This is because of the problems of interfacing (connecting all systems together) and because of the disruption which would occur if one part of the system malfunctioned which could bring the system as a whole to a standstill.

Figure 3.1 portrays an example of an integrated system representative of the real world consisting of many interrelated sub-systems such as sales order processing, warehousing and despatching of orders, sales invoicing and sales accounting to which is added marketing, production planning and stock control. This assumes that when orders are despatched goods need to be replenished either by internal manufacturing processes or from outside suppliers. When functions are related in this way a foundation is provided for their integration into a larger more efficient system avoiding the need to input the same data to several related functional systems. A wages system requires the input of data relating to hours worked and/or units produced as a basis for calculating wages. A costing system requires the same data for charging jobs and contracts or for comparing actual wages costs with standard costs. Instead of duplicating the data it is only necessary to transfer the details to the costing function for analysis purposes to assess the cost applicable to jobs, contracts and overhead expenses to which wages data could be updated.

3.2.1 Integrated software packages

Integrated software packages go some way to attaining the ideal integrated system because the various modules are directly related and can be interfaced allowing data from one to be passed to the other. Integrated software consists of a set of programs for performing related functional processes. A typical integrated accounting package consists of sales, purchase and nominal ledger to which may be added sales invoicing or order processing. Stock control and payroll modules can also be added to provide a highly integrated accounting system. The input of data only need be done once and all relevant accounts are updated automatically. For example, when issuing an invoice to a customer the stock items on the invoice will automatically reduce the quantity in stock. The entries are also automatically entered in the nominal ledger.

3.2.2 Financial and non-financial systems

Business systems fall into two main categories – financial and non-financial. Financial systems include payroll processing; purchase and sales accounting; budgetary control, cost control, credit control, cash flow control and capital expenditure control; asset accounting, administration of investment portfolios and hiring and/or leasing of motor vehicles, computers and other assets, etc. Non-financial systems include marketing and selling; stock control and production planning and control; purchasing; building and plant maintenance systems; administrative systems relating to personnel, hotel accommodation, holiday bookings and airline seat reservations, etc. It must be appreciated, however, that some non-financial systems have financial elements. For example, a system dealing with hotel accommodation has to provide for payments by guests, with details being transferred to the accounting system. Similarly, a holiday booking system primarily concerned with accommodation and seat reservations must be linked to a financial system which deals with deposits, refunds and final payments for holidays by clients.

3.3 CONTROL SYSTEMS

Many business systems are control systems which monitor and modify the use of resources of related systems. For example, the production control system is interfaced with manufacturing activities in the factory with responsibility for progressing jobs throughout all processes and operations. Other examples are provided below. A control system may be defined as 'A control loop super-imposed upon a physical system to form a composite system with in-built mechanisms for the detection of variations in the behaviour of the system. Such variations provide the basis for taking corrective action to maintain stability in the system while achieving predefined performance parameters.' This definition will be analysed within the following text. Examples of systems subject to control and their related control system(s) are shown in Box 3.2.

System controlled	Control system
Manufacturing	1. Production control
	2. Quality control
	3. Cost control
	4. Budgetary control
	5. Project control
	6. Operational controls
Administration	1. Credit control
	2. Stock control
	3. Budgetary control
Accounting	1. Audit control
	2. Capital expenditure control
	3. Control of assets
	4. Control accounts
	5. Cash control
	6. Financial controls
	7. Budgetary control
Systems development	1. Project control
	2. Version control
	3. Quality control
	4. Budgetary control
Marketing and sales	1. Finished stock control
	2. Order control
	3. Budgetary control
	4. Sales quota control
Information processing	1. Operational controls
	2. Batch controls
	3. Quality control
	4. Budgetary control

Box 3.2 Control examples

Note that the terms difference, variation, variance, deviation and error effectively mean the same thing – they are synonyms. Budgetary control and standard costing systems tend to use the term variance in respect of differences between actual and budgeted overheads. The term error is used in the context of cybernetics to mean the difference between actual results relating to the controlled variable, such as the level of sales or production, and the reference input, i.e. predefined performance parameters. The remaining terms – difference, variation and deviation – are used in a general way.

3.3.1 Control interface

Control systems are linked to other related systems by the flow of data from one to the other. The flow of data may be considered to be the control interface which triggers off the control process. When data is input for processing by computer the input device may be classified as the interface because it joins the external system to the computer system by a cable or communication line. Devices in this category include terminal keyboards, factory data recorders, auto teller terminals and point of sale terminals.

Negative feedback

Feedback is the process of communicating a systems output, such as number of units sold of a specified product, to the control system for comparison with the number of units targeted. This is for the purpose of detecting deviations as a basis for modifying the status of the system to attain a state of equilibrium, i.e. to achieve predefined objectives. Most business control systems are negative, error-actuated systems because when the actual and expected behaviours of a system are compared any differences are detected as positive deviations. Corrective action is effected in the opposite direction to counteract them to bring the system back to a stable state. For example, if overhead expenditure exceeds the amount allowed in the budget it is detected as a positive or unfavourable variance. Action needs to be taken to reduce the level of overhead which requires an adjustment in the opposite direction to the variance – hence the terms negative and error-actuated.

Positive feedback

Positive feedback has the opposite effect to negative feedback and may be applied when it is deemed appropriate to amplify a variance or error. Positive feedback is applicable when resources, such as raw materials or consumable supplies, are obtained below budgeted or standard price. Management would wish to take advantage of this situation and so take action to purchase more resources at advantageous prices. Similar considerations apply when using more efficient methods than those established as standard. In this respect a change of method would probably be implemented which becomes the new standard thereby eliminating variances.

Feedforward

Error signals are variances from planned performance which are used to modify the current state of a system. If a record of such variances is maintained over a period of time, then that record may be used as a basis for setting future system control parameters, particularly if those in current use are erroneous and/or impractical of achievement. The future state of the system may then be estimated, potential problems and opportunities identified, and suitable action taken. The data is fed forward in time and is used to make predictions of what is to occur, leading to the description feedforward control.

3.3.2 The exception principle

Many control systems function on what is referred to as the *exception principle*, the basis of *management by exception*. An exception is a deviation from planned performance or variation in the behaviour of the system from predefined performance parameters. The importance of the exception principle is that only significant facts are reported to management or operational staff as a basis for taking action to maintain the system in a stable state. The technique avoids having to supply managers with many pages of printout for scrutiny to detect situations which require the application of corrective measures. When searching through large printouts it is an easy matter to overlook items because of either interruptions or fatigue. Or the search may take so long that the situation to which the information relates has changed and is no longer valid. It is not a manager's job to search for significant information, rather the responsibility of the information systems to provide it in the form it is required. Examples of control systems applying the exception principle include budgetary control, standard costing, stock control and credit control, etc.

Pareto's Law

Related to the exception principle is Pareto's Law, which says that many business situations have an 80/20 characteristic. This is best explained by examples, for instance:

1.   80% of orders are obtained from 20% of customers.
2.   80% of project benefits are obtained from 20% of the projects undertaken.
3.   80% of the value of stocks is represented by 20% of the items in stock.
4.   80% of invoice errors will be in 20% of the invoices.
5.   80% of profits are obtained from 20% of the product range.
6.   80% of cost variances will be incurred by 20% of items produced.
7.   80% of overhead variances will be incurred by 20% of the overheads.

Note that in real situations, the ratios may deviate from 80/20; 70/30 or 90/10 or other values are possible, depending on how the analysis is carried out. The significance of Pareto's law is that the extent to which control is applied may be reduced by concentrating on the smaller element of the relevant object, function or activity under control. Less rigid control procedures may then be applied to the larger element.

3.3.3 Cybernetics

It is impossible to discuss control systems without recourse to the science of cybernetics. The word cybernetics was coined by Norbert Wiener from the Greek word *kubernetes*, a derivative of the Latin word *gubernator*, which may be translated to mean governor or controller. The term governor is used in many instances, for example The Governor of the Bank of England is the controller of the bank's affairs; a prison governor responsible for controlling all prison activities; governing bodies presiding over the affairs of schools and colleges and so on. Colloquially the term governor may be interpreted to mean the boss or the person in overall charge of operations. Cybernetics is the study of control processes in electronic, mechanical and biological systems, particularly with regard to the analysis of the information flows within them. Cybernetic systems have built-in sensory devices for measuring the magnitude of the output – the actual state – of a system. The measured output is compared with a reference input specifying control parameters defining the required state of the system. The difference between the two states is a measure of the variance or error which is communicated to an effector as a basis for adjusting the controlled variable to attain a state of homeostasis. See Box 3.3 and Figure 3.2 for more details of the cybernetic control process.

3.3.4 Cybernetic principles applied to a budgetary control system

Budgetary control systems embrace all business functions, including functional expenditure budgets; sales, production and capital expenditure budgets, etc. Every function utilises resources during the course of its activities, including manpower (or should it be person power?), consumable materials and overhead expenses. A budgetary control system is designed to control the use of these resources. Such systems are implemented in many businesses to provide information on budgeted and actual levels of sales, production and stocks; production, administration, research and development and selling and marketing overheads. The actual results are compared with budgets for computing variances. This is a management by exception technique which highlights significant variances indicating the areas needing corrective action.

Budgeted and actual overheads are usually recorded on a form such as a department summary sheet. It lists the various classes of expenditure including

1. Reference input	The planned use of resources relevant to a specific system for a stated time. It may called a target, standard, objective or budget, e.g. the volume (quantity) of a particular product to be sold each week, the amount of credit allowed to customers, the standard price of a material or component part, the standard time allowed for a specified manufacturing operation using standard methods, and so on.
2. Sensor	A device for measuring the magnitude of a variable indicating the actual state of the system, e.g. a counter is a sensor when connected to, say, a power press in a factory and it is incremented after each cycle of the machine indicating the number of items processed. A sensor can also be a person in a control system responsible for observing the status of a controlled variable, e.g. the account balances of customers.
3. Feedback	The output signal from the sensor is communicated by the process of feedback to the comparator.
4. Comparator	A device in a system for detecting the difference between the actual state of a system and the desired state of a system represented by the reference input. A comparator in a credit control system may be a clerk or a segment of a computer program comparing account balances with the allowed credit limit.
5. Error signal	The difference between the magnitude of the controlled variable and the reference input, the error signal is communicated to an effector.
6. Effector	A device which responds to error signals received from the comparator by modifying the behaviour of the system to achieve the defined level of performance as set by the reference input. The device may be a person such as a supervisor or manager. The action taken depends upon the nature of the controlled variables. Examples include increasing production to offset shortfalls, increasing sales by additional advertising to increase demand to attain the desired sales value or improving material handling procedures to avoid excessive waste of materials.
7. Modify	New targets or objectives may be set to allow for changes in the prevailing situation.

Box 3.3 Cybernetic control processes

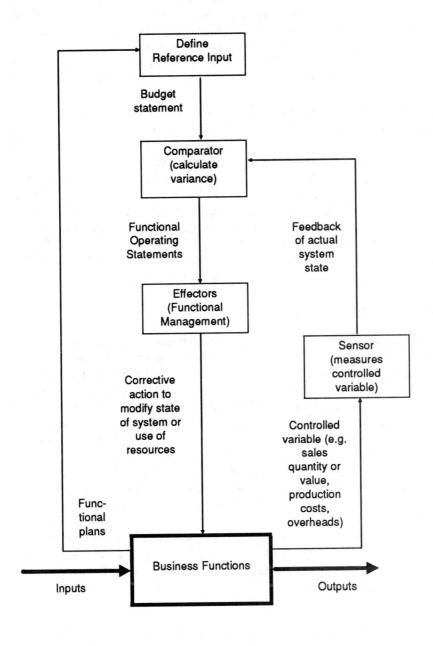

Figure 3.2 Budgetary control system

operating labour, general operating overheads, consumable supplies and details relating to equipment such as depreciation, leasing, and maintenance costs. Expenditure relating to service departments and general overheads is also recorded. Columns are provided for budget, actual and variances both for the current month and the year to date. A monthly summary sheet is prepared and issued to each department and used as a basis for taking action to eliminate adverse variances.

Figure 3.2 illustrates the action of a budgetary control system applying cybernetic principles. Reference inputs are established initially in the form of budgets indicating the policy to be pursued during the specified period. The reference inputs are expressed in terms of the relevant controlled variable such as sales quantity and value, production quantities and costs, operating costs and/or overheads. A sensor collects details of the results, i.e. the magnitude of the controlled variable, which are communicated by the process of feedback to a comparator. The actual state of the system is then compared with the reference inputs and the variances are recorded on functional operating statements which are issued to the relevant managers, the effectors, for taking corrective action to modify the state of the system and the use of resources.

3.3.5 Cost control

Many manufacturing organisations produce standard products from standard components and implement standard costing systems to control their cost. Standard costs are determined for direct labour based on standard operation times and standard rates of pay. The standard cost of direct material is computed on the basis of a standard material or bought-out component specifications and a predetermined standard price. Deviations of actual costs from standard costs are analysed to provide information on an exception basis. Adverse and favourable variances are analysed as to their cause. In respect of materials or parts, variances often relate to price differences from standard, i.e. paying more or less than standard price due to various reasons. One reason may be due to obtaining supplies from an alternative supplier in an emergency at higher than standard price. Other variances occur due to excessive usage reflecting the incidence of rejects or careless handling of materials. Variances also occur due to variations of efficiency in performing tasks resulting in actual hours in excess of, or less than, standard. Variances can also occur because of method changes, such as using different tools or machines.

3.4 EXECUTIVE INFORMATION SYSTEMS (EISs)

Business management is a complex task requiring the use of information as a strategic tool by the entire executive team. EIS software facilitates this requirement by providing information for decision support to attain a competitive advantage. This is achieved by the more effective use of information for determining strategies which are ultimately expressed in an improved profit figure. An executive does not require keyboard skills to use an EIS because provision is made for using a mouse, a touch screen, or a special controller (like a TV remote control) for performing EIS functions. An executive selects the desired report or chart and the information is displayed on the screen in just a few seconds. The displayed reports can be accompanied by colour charts showing important trends.

Details are provided in Box 3.4 of Commander-EIS, marketed by Comshare Ltd. This is a typical EIS available in the UK.

3.4.1 Features of an executive information system

Such a system is designed to make strategic information readily available to senior executives whilst minimising the workload of the information providers who support the executive team. It automates the processes which are required for the successful implementation of an EIS. These are information access, integration, analysis, reporting and delivery.

User views

Different executives have different views of an organisation and hence of its data. For example, production executives have different information needs from finance people. However, each executive should be able to specify those items of information which are important. Corporate standards can then define the range of information classified as being significant. The points or levels at which remedial action is necessary can be preset and the range modified for personal sensitivity requirements. Information can be provided in respect of business performance not only in traditional profit and loss structures but in other ways suitable for managerial control. Information may be analysed by business or operating unit, product group or line, distribution channel, geographical area, customer group or classification and so on. Any one of these views can be selected to provide the best perspective for establishing the existence of a problem or an opportunity requiring executive action.

Multiple levels of analysis

An executive who has identified a significant variance needs to view the data from a number of different perspectives. It is not enough to know that at the

Commander Executive Workstation runs on many models of PC and consists of the Briefing Book, Newswire, Execu-View, Redi-mail and Reminder.

Briefing Book	The briefing book provides key information to executives electronically. Numeric reports, charts, text or documents may be combined to provide a series of menu-driven briefing screens. Each executive can have a personalised selection of reports and charts relevant to his responsibilities.
Newswire	In addition to internal information, management also require up-to-date information from external sources relating to stock prices, exchange rates and general economic and industrial news. Menus make it easy to select and display the required information.
Execu-View	An invaluable aid to executives who find that standard reports do not provide them with enough information and who wish to investigate further, Execu-View offers a graphic interface which can be used to create the multiple perspectives needed to respond to executives' needs for strategic information.
Redi-mail	Handles electronic mail via a user-friendly interface.
Reminder	Provides a calendar and diary facility.

System W/DSS is a decision support system which provides a spreadsheet-oriented investigative capability without using commands or syntax. Features include analytical facilities – multi-dimensional allocations; solving simultaneous equations, statistical forecasting, reporting and business graphics, etc. Up to nine dimensions are supported providing the ability to manage many spreadsheets. Included are Datman, Pipelines and File Power to enable access to data from multiple, incompatible sources. One-up is a stand-alone multi-dimensional spreadsheet for modelling and analysis. System W/DSS can be accessed via Execu-View.

Workstation Manager is mainframe based and manages information flows to both Executive and Builder workstations, which may be distributed throughout an organisation. Information may be in the form of reports, charts, spreadsheets, programs, models, data files or other documents. It has facilities for automatic checking for errors in communications and facilitating re-transmission and automatic cataloguing and downloading to the PC.

Box 3.4 Features of an EIS

group or consolidated level of operations an unfavourable profit variance of 5% has occurred. Some operating units may have increased profits while others have profit deviations in excess of 5% so it is important to obtain information on these factors. It is necessary to analyse information more deeply, not only pinpointing the magnitude of the profit deviations in the different operating areas, but to establish the root cause of the deviations. Deviations from planned performance may be due to any number of reasons depending upon the nature of the business, the extent of competition and the general state of the economy. A detailed analysis may indicate that the situation is caused by a shortage of key raw materials causing a cutback in production below the level of sales demand. The root cause may also be competitors reducing their selling prices.

An EIS supports multiple levels of investigation. By selecting a highlighted variance on the screen it is possible to obtain more detail of its underlying cause(s), drilling down through the layers of information to, say, an explanatory memo which can be displayed on the screen. Individual items in a report can be selected like menu choices with higher level report values pointing to lower levels of details.

3.4.2 Benefits of using an executive information system

The creation of an EIS provides the opportunity to identify important information, enabling the attention of executives to be focused on critical operational areas. This analysis alone can often justify the effort of implementing an EIS. After implementation critical information becomes available on demand, reducing the volume of routine information which must be sifted to detect critical facts requiring managerial attention. Speedy access to information is facilitated electronically, e.g. information is available from computerised data processing systems and databases by exchanging data between mainframe and other computers. The use of colour graphics is an important feature of EISs and highlights significant variances or patterns in the figures displayed.

3.5 REVISION NOTES

1.   An information system is a system which collects, records, stores, compares and computes data in respect of business transactions which then becomes meaningful information.
2.   All information systems consist of four primary elements; these are input, processing, storage and output.
3.   The elements of a computer system are similar to those listed in note 2

above. They consist of an input device, a processor, a storage device and an output device.

4. An integrated system consists of interrelated functions whereby information produced as output from one provides input to another.

5. The total systems approach to systems development recognises that all business systems when combined form a complete business entity as opposed to viewing them as self-contained isolated systems.

6. The piecemeal approach develops individual systems without considering how they relate to others in the organisation.

7. Integrated software packages consist of modules which can be interfaced facilitating the transfer of data from one to another, e.g. when producing an invoice the value of the invoice will update the customer's account in the sales ledger module and reduce the quantity in stock of each item sold in the stock control module.

8. A prerequisite of any effective information system is its ability to access information regardless of where or how it is stored. A system is required which integrates different computers running on different operating systems, both internal and external, into a single unified computing and information resource. The means of accomplishing this is by open system architecture.

9. Many business systems monitor and modify the use of resources of related systems. A control system is in effect a feedback control loop superimposed upon a physical system, e.g. the production control system controls production activities by means of variances. Refer to note 10 and feedback in note 12.

10. Control is achieved by comparing results with plans and any deviations in the behaviour of the system are detected as variances. The terms difference, deviation, variance, variation or error (cybernetic term for deviation) are synonyms.

11. Control systems are connected (interfaced) to related systems by the flow of data from one to the other. This is accomplished in a computer system by connecting an input device to the processor which provides an interface between the two devices. In effect this interfaces the production control function with the production function. The production control program would then compare actual results with targets and produce a variance report.

12. Feedback is the process of communicating a systems output to the control system for comparison with the controlled variable to establish variances as a basis for modifying the status of the system.

13. There are two types of feedback – negative and positive. Most businesses are negative error-actuated systems applying negative feedback to correct differences which are detected as positive deviations. Positive feedback has

the opposite effect to negative feedback and is applied to amplify a variance.

14. The exception principle is the basis of management by exception whereby the exceptions are deviations from planned results. Only significant facts, i.e. exceptions to normal, such as insurance premiums due but not yet paid, are reported upon.

15. Cybernetics is the study of control processes in man and machine systems.

16. Cybernetic systems use reference inputs which are control parameters for controlling a specific system. The parameters can be described as targets, standards, objects or budgets and may be expressed in terms of quantities produced, the number of units sold, the credit limit allowed to customers or the budgeted amount of overheads, etc.

17. Cybernetic systems have built-in sensory devices for measuring the magnitude of a systems output signal. The output signal is the controlled variable which indicates the actual state of the system. The magnitude of the output signal must be expressed in similar terms to the reference input indicated in note 16.

18. A comparator is a manual or automatic device in a machine or computer program for detecting the difference between two states – the magnitude of the controlled variable (the actual state of the system) and the reference input (the desired state of the system).

19. An effector is an automatic device or person which responds to error signals (variances) received from the control system by taking appropriate action to maintain a state of homeostasis.

20. Homeostasis is the process of attaining stability in systems when affected by internal and external environmental influences by taking the most appropriate corrective action.

21. Executive information systems provide strategic information to management by providing the best perspective of business activities whether relating to product groups, geographical areas, customer classifications and so on. The EIS allows an executive who has identified a significant variance to analyse the information more deeply to establish an underlying cause. The variance may apply to a reduction in sales of a specified product. Digging deeper may indicate that a specific customer is placing orders for lower quantities due to a fall-off of demand or it may be due to a competitor coming into the market.

3.6 SELF-TEST QUESTIONS

1. Briefly describe the characteristics of an information system, indicating its four primary elements.

2. What is the primary feature of an integrated system?
3. Distinguish between the 'total systems approach' and the 'piecemeal approach' to systems development.
4. What are integrated software packages and what benefits do they provide to a business?
5. A prerequisite of an effective information system is its ability to access information regardless of where or how it is stored. Discuss.
6. What are the primary features of a control system? How is control achieved?
7. What are variances and what part do they play in business control?
8. Distinguish between negative and positive feedback.
9. State the underlying concept of the 'exception principle'.
10. What is meant by the term 'cybernetics'?
11. Explain the meaning of EACH of the following terms:
    (a) reference inputs;
    (b) sensory device;
    (c) comparator;
    (d) effector;
    (e) homeostasis.
12. What are the principal features of an executive information system?

3.7 FURTHER READING

1. *Business Systems and Information Technology*, Ron Anderson, Paradigm/Blackwell Scientific Publications: Oxford, 1988. Refer to chapter 4.
2. *Information and Management Systems, Concepts and applications*, Mike Harry, Pitman: London, 1990. Refer to chapters 3 and 4.
3. *Business Information Systems*, Chris Clare and Peri Loucopoulos, Paradigm/Blackwell Scientific Publications: Oxford, 1987. Refer to chapter 1.

Chapter 4

Accounting systems

INTRODUCTION AND SUMMARY

The accounting function usually consists of two main activities – financial accounting and management accounting. Financial accounting is responsible for the custodianship of a company's assets and for maintaining statutory records relating to national insurance deductions, PAYE and VAT, etc. It is also responsible for ensuring that transactions are recorded in proper books of account, for the effective operation of all accounting activities and for implementing internal check procedures, in conjunction with an internal audit department (if one exists).

Accounting systems, whether manual or computerised, can be analysed into two types – cashbook systems and ledger systems. Both systems analyse income (receipts) and expenditure (payments) to different categories which are eventually summarised to produce reports, a trial balance, a profit and loss account and a balance sheet. This chapter covers the principles of financial accounting systems as implemented on small business computers and looks at some of the problems associated with using common software for this purpose.

The management accounting function is responsible for the preparation and distribution of operational and financial information to the various functions for control purposes. This includes the reporting of excess manufacturing costs incurred in the factory and comparing the operating costs incurred with the budgeted allowance for the level of activity achieved. The management accounting function is also responsible for preparing cash flow statements, profit projections, balance sheet forecasts and the preparation of functional budgets. In addition, management accounting evaluates capital expenditure projects and analyses the balance sheet and profit and loss account to provide key financial ratios including return on capital employed, return on operating assets, gross and net profit margin on sales, turnover of assets, asset utilisation, current ratio and liquidity ratio, etc. These statistics are vital for managerial control as they provide a basis of comparison with company targets for applying corrective action. The further study of management accounting systems is beyond the scope of this book.

4.1 THE EVOLUTION OF ACCOUNTING SYSTEMS

The expression *proper books of account* at one time implied the use of bound ledgers, one page or more being allocated to each account. This type of ledger was subsequently replaced, in many instances, by loose leaf ledgers. Separate ledgers were used for each class of account such as sales ledger, purchase ledger and stock ledger.

When electromechanical accounting and bookkeeping machines came into use ledger cards were used for recording account details. They were made out of stiff board to withstand frequent handling in and out of the machine for recording transactions. Transactions were posted (recorded or updated) by keyboard instead of manually. Ledger cards were subsequently replaced with punched cards when appropriate equipment, manufactured by companies such as Hollerith and Powers-Samas, was installed in the larger business. Transaction and account details were recorded on punched cards – one card for each transaction and one for each record. A pack of punched cards containing details of, say, stock transactions formed a transaction file. A pack of punched cards storing details of customer accounts became the sales ledger or sales ledger master file. A similar method was used when punched card oriented computers became available.

As the electronic computer was further developed the punched card system was replaced, in some instances, with computers which use magnetic cards for storing account details. The cards were referred to as card random access memory (CRAM). A file of cards was housed in a magazine which was accessed to obtain details of a specific record by notches cut in the top and bottom edges of each card. The notches were used for the mechanical selection of a card from the magazine. Selected cards were transported along a card feed track to the read/write station.

Transactions and records are now predominantly stored on some type of magnetic disk or diskette. Printed details of transaction files and master files stored on magnetic disk are obtained by printing out the contents of the magnetic file. The printouts are stored in binders and serve the same purpose as earlier bound ledgers and day books. The wheel has turned full circle!

4.1.1 Organisational aspects of the accounting function

Prior to the implementation of capital intensive electromechanical punched card equipment the accounting department performed accounting routines for many functions of the business. These included updating the sales, purchase and stock ledgers, etc. With the advent of the punched card equipment, however, the routines were transferred to the centralised machine room, as it was often called, in order to utilise fully the capital investment in the punched card system.

The same situation applied with the implementation of large mainframe computers which superseded the earlier electromechanical punched card equipment. Most accounting systems were transferred to a centralised data processing (DP) department responsible for running the computer installation and under the control of a data processing manager. In this respect the DP department acted as a service department processing the data of most of the business functions in the same way as the earlier machine room. Although the processing of accounting data was carried out by a separate and independent department, the accounting function still had ultimate responsibility for the effective dissemination of accounting information and advising personnel of the manner of its interpretation.

Currently many accounting departments employ small business computers or multi-access terminal-based systems to process accounting applications within the department. Once again the accounting department is responsible for the processing of accounting data.

4.2 CASHBOOK ACCOUNTING SYSTEMS

A cashbook system is likely to be used by small businesses which receive direct cash payments for the services or products they provide. Businesses such as sweet shops, book shops and newsagents (apart from weekly payments for paper deliveries) and petrol stations (unless operating credit sales for specific customers) do not normally provide facilities for credit sales. Consequently the need for invoices does not arise as sales are recorded using till receipts. Transactions are either receipts or payments which are analysed and recorded in the respective columns of a cashbook which represent the movement of cash in and out of the bank account.

When using cashbook software each transaction is specifically coded for purposes of analysis. Different codes may be used to distinguish between different categories of sales. A garage, for instance, typically analyses sales into petrol, oil, accessories, music cassettes and various oddments such as garden furniture, watches and birthday cards, etc. Expenses would be similarly analysed and coded by type of expense such as telephone, postage and stationery, heating and lighting, maintenance, insurance, wages or salaries, payments to the Department of Social Security for national insurance, to the Customs and Excise for value-added tax and to the Inland Revenue for income tax deducted from employees' pay.

Income from sales is effectively a debit to the bank account and a credit to the sales account; expenses are credit transactions in the bank account. The opposite entry is a debit to the respective expense account. At the end of the accounting period, usually each month, cashbook columns are totalled to provide figures for preparing a profit and loss account and balance sheet. These details are already available on disk if using a software package. Unpaid expenses do not of course enter the cashbook until they are paid. In this case the unpaid expenses are taken into account as accruals and appear in the balance sheet as a liability. Payments in advance are entered in the cashbook and need to be adjusted so that the current accounts only carry a charge for the portion of the expenses incurred. This applies to insurance premiums and other similar expenses paid for the whole year. The unexpired portion of an expense is recorded in the balance sheet as an asset. Computerised cashbooks perform all of these functions together with an audit trail.

4.3 LEDGER ACCOUNTING SYSTEMS

Manual ledger systems used by businesses to process large volumes of transactions are very ponderous to operate, mainly because of the need to enter transaction details several times. For example, details of credit sales to customers need first of all to be recorded on invoices which are then used as a basis for summarising all daily sales in the sales daybook. Entries are then made to the relevant customer's account in the sales ledger. Details of the total sales are then posted as a debit entry to the sales ledger control account (or debtor control account) in the nominal ledger. The net sales value (excluding VAT) is entered as a credit entry to the sales account and the VAT on sales is entered as a credit to the VAT control account, again in the nominal ledger. If any transaction entry is overlooked or incorrectly recorded, the ledger will not balance. Some time may then be needed to discover and correct the discrepancies.

The principle of entering the data in two ways (debits and credits) is known as *double entry bookkeeping*. The techniques of double entry accounting were developed around 500 years ago in Venice and although the technology has changed, the approach is still recognisably the same. The major advantage of the approach is ease of checking to help detect and prevent mistakes and fraud. Also, in manual systems the work was spread over several staff who would have to collude to make a mistake or change undetectable. Accounting software performs the functions of double entry bookkeeping automatically, freeing the accountant to concentrate on the interpretation of the information or allowing some organisations to dispense with trained bookkeepers for day-to-day work. Data is entered via the keyboard once and the software makes the appropriate postings to the relevant ledger accounts. The need for the user to consider debits and credits disappears. The production of a trial balance – a list of the balances remaining on each account – is the work of a few minutes in all but the largest systems. Discrepancies can be detected automatically, although most software is now so developed that errors and inconsistencies cannot be posted into the system. Rather they are rejected by the error checking and data validation features of the programs. Note, however, that this presupposes that the programs cannot be altered. If a programmer is allowed to alter the system, then any or all of the safety features can be overridden, creating the conditions for major errors or fraud. This is one reason why programmers are often not allowed to work with real systems, instead having to work with dummy data.

The rest of this section will look at each of the principal ledgers in the typical accounting system – sales, purchase and nominal (or general) ledgers.

4.3.1 Sales accounting systems

The sales accounting system is built around a sales ledger, a list of customer accounts. It is normal trade practice to supply goods on credit to customers deemed to be credit worthy. Figure 4.1 illustrates a typical sales accounting routine, described in more detail below.

Details of credit sales are recorded on an invoice including for each different item the stock number or commodity code, description, price, value of the goods, postage or transportation costs and VAT. The invoice value is debited to the relevant customer's account in the sales ledger. The value of goods returned is credited to the respective customer's account. Invoices are recorded in a sales daybook and sales returns are recorded in a returns book or printed on a transaction list if it is a computerised application. The total value of sales excluding VAT is credited to the sales account, VAT is credited to the VAT account and the total sales value is debited to the debtor control account in the nominal ledger. The total value of sales returns less VAT is debited to the sales account (or sales returns account), VAT is debited to the VAT account and the total value of returns is credited to the debtor control account. Remittances from customers are debited to the bank account and credited to the debtor control account in the nominal ledger. Specific remittances from customers are credited to their relevant accounts in the sales ledger.

At the end of the trading month statements of account are prepared for each customer which may show an aged account balance. An aged debtors report may also be produced showing how much of the account owed (the balance) by each customer has been outstanding for one month, two months, three months and over. This information is valuable for credit control. *Balance-forward* statements do not itemise the invoices or other debits comprising the opening balance. *Open item* statements record all debits and credits and indicate how remittances have been allocated so that customers are more easily able to reconcile the amount outstanding with their own records.

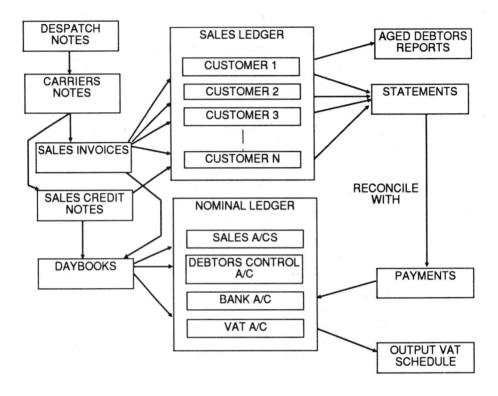

Figure 4.1 Sales accounting system

A sales analysis is prepared for sales management which may show sales for the current month analysed by product group, sales area, customer and representative, etc. An audit trail is produced listing all the transactions for the period. Remittances received, but which are unmatched with sales invoices, are recorded on an unallocated cash report. If a remittance cannot be made to a specific invoice it is normal practice to allocate it to the oldest outstanding transaction.

4.3.2 Purchase accounting systems

The purchase accounting system is built around the purchase ledger, a list of supplier accounts. It is normal trade practice to buy goods on credit from suppliers. A typical purchase accounting procedure is shown in Figure 4.2 and is described in greater detail below.

Goods received from suppliers are normally credit purchases which are charged on purchase invoices. Delivery notes are sent by the supplier with the goods. The goods receiving section records details of the goods on goods received notes which are used for recording receipts on stock records. Each purchase invoice is reconciled with the purchase order, goods received note, debit note(s) for returns and delivery note to ensure that there are no discrepancies. The reconciled purchase invoices are recorded in a purchase day-book or printed on a transaction list. The suppliers' accounts are updated with the value of the goods received. The total value of purchases excluding VAT is debited to the purchase account (analysed by purchase analysis code), VAT is debited to the VAT account and the total value of purchases is credited to the creditor control account in the nominal ledger. The total value of purchase returns less VAT is credited to the VAT account and the total value of returns is debited to the creditor control account.

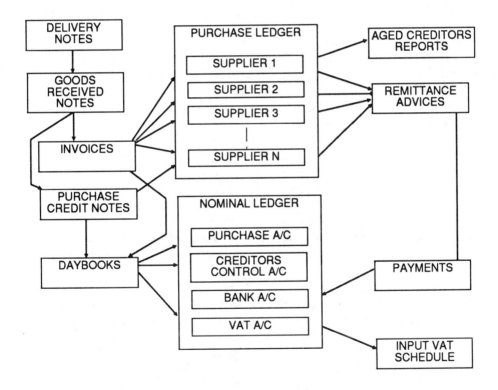

Figure 4.2 Purchase accounting system

A purchase analysis is prepared for accounting and budgetary control purposes by classification codes allocated to each type of purchase or charge for services. In a computerised system a *chart of accounts* (see Section 4.3.3 below) is prepared allocating each type of expense to a specified code. The code is recorded for each item when posted. This allows a nominal ledger to be analysed by expense groups and sub-groups.

Statements of account are received from suppliers at the end of the trading month and the outstanding balance (amount owing) is reconciled with the balance shown by the suppliers' accounts in the purchase ledger. Suppliers' accounts are then inspected to decide which should be paid in full and those for which part payments are to be made. Appropriate remittances are then made, together with remittance advice notes, either by bank giro transfer, cheque or BACS (the Bankers Automated Clearing System, which allows the electronic tranfer of funds between bank accounts). The total remittances are credited to the bank account and debited to the creditor control account in the nominal ledger which then records the current total amount owing to suppliers. Details of transactions are recorded in a daybook or printed on a transaction list providing an audit trail.

As with sales, details of the purchase accounting system may be analysed to show inputs, outputs and the nature of the files and accounts used in the system. Once again this is useful information for anyone concerned with the development of systems.

4.3.3 Nominal ledger systems

This ledger is also a series of accounts, but this time they are not 'personal' accounts relating to a customer or supplier. Instead it is a series of accounts in which the expenses, assets and liabilities are recorded.

Expenses are payments made by a company for goods and services which are consumed rather than traded. The expenses represent expenditure on items which are essential to the operation of the company but which are not directly part of that operation. Examples are rent, rates, lighting and heating, advertising, fees, etc. These are sometimes called *overheads*. Assets are amounts owed to the company and the value of items owned by an organisation. The usual examples are land, buildings, machinery, vehicles, debtors, etc. Liabilities are amounts owed to others. Examples are creditors, loans, shareholdings, etc.

The accounts are grouped so that details of related income or expenses are held together. A coding system which highlights the groups is used to name each account, creating a *chart of accounts*. Box 4.1 shows part of a typical chart of accounts for a small company.

The nominal ledger also contains the information to produce three key accounting reports:

Group Number	Description	Account Number	Description
1	Sales	100	Sales
		101	Sales returns
2	Cost of sales	200	Direct wages
		201	Direct materials
		202	Direct expenses
3	Expenses – travel	300	Petrol & oil
		301	Road tax & insurance
		302	Repairs & servicing
		303	Air & rail costs
4	Expenses – general	400	Property
		401	Medical
		402	Equipment
5	Expenses – selling & advertising	500 . . .	etc.
6	Expenses – professional charges		
7	Expenses – wages & salaries		
8	Expenses – bank interest & charges		

Box 4.1 Nominal code structure

Trial balance – a list of the outstanding balances in the nominal ledger, including the sum of all debtors and the sum of all creditors, at a specified point in time. In traditional manual systems, this was produced at the end of each period (usually a month) as a prelude to producing a profit and loss account. Many accounting packages allow this to be produced at any time in a few minutes.

Trading and profit and loss accounts – these two accounts summarise the income and expense for a business over a period – monthly, quarterly, annually.

Balance sheet – this is a list of the assets and liabilities of a company at a specified point in time. It is usually produced by accounting packages automatically along with a profit and loss account.

The nominal ledger is the hub of the accounting system – around it revolves all the financial transactions and records of the company. The nominal ledger shows what happens to the money belonging to the company – the sales that have been made, the purchases made, the expenses incurred, the value of stock, the amount of money (called depreciation) set aside to cover the fall in value of the company's assets (plant, machinery, vehicles, etc.).

Most of the entries in a nominal ledger are posted from the sales and purchase ledgers, but some payments and receipts do not easily fit sales or purchases. In these cases, entries are made via the journal, a method of recording transfers between accounts in a nominal ledger. The journal is used to correct mistakes, record transfers and deal with special items such as disposal of assets.

4.4 ACCOUNTING SOFTWARE PACKAGES

Every business needs to prepare accounts, from the one-man business to the multi-national corporation. The smaller business requires less complex accounting systems than the large business but the primary principles of accounting are still relevant. Packages are available to suit the needs of all types and size of business by harnessing the power of a computer to perform the mundane tasks associated with accounting routines. A major advantage of using computer-based accounting packages is that the double entry aspect is largely transparent to the user. This is because in some packages a transaction entered on an invoice automatically updates the sales ledger, stock account and nominal ledger. Many packages provide for single- and multi-user requirements and include record locking facilities. See Chapter 5 for more details of these technical issues.

Accounting packages sometimes consist of modules which may be run individually or may be integrated for the purpose of increasing the effectiveness of the accounting system. Typical modules include sales ledger, invoicing, purchase ledger, stock control, payroll and nominal ledger. Options provided by typical modules are shown in Box 4.2.

Notice that all ledgers have similar facilities including those for creating and maintaining master files, parameter maintenance, account enquiries and transaction listing, etc. The various ledgers then deal specifically with specialised accounting matters. In particular, notice the close resemblance of the sales and purchase ledger facilities (see Figures 4.1 and 4.2). The primary difference is that sales are income generating transactions and purchases are expenditure generating transactions – the opposite but similar types of transaction processing.

Nominal ledger module

. File creation   . Parameter maintenance
. File maintenance   . Master file print
. Journal posting   . Account enquiries
. Accruals posting   . Prepayments posting
. Trial balance   . Transaction report
. Financial reports   . Consolidation

Purchase ledger module

. File creation   . Parameter maintenance
. File maintenance   . Master file print
. Batch posting   . Payments
. Aged creditors report   . Account enquiry
. Transaction listing   . Remittance print
. VAT print   . Month-end update

Box 4.2 Typical accounting module features

4.4.1 Acquiring a package

There are three typical sources of accounting software for the smaller company which wishes to use computer-based accounting, namely local suppliers, mail-order suppliers and shareware (see Box 4.3). However, whichever type of supplier is chosen, it is usually necessary to justify the acquisition, i.e. to consider whether the money to be spent on the system will be recouped from

The term shareware may be described as a concept whereby the authors of software (application or utility programs) retain all rights to it under copyright laws but allow distribution of their programs to be done freely or with few restrictions. If the software is used, however, the user is expected to register it with the author for a stated registration fee. In return the author often provides a bound manual, telephone support, free updates and more powerful versions. It is interesting to note that shareware is very popular and successful in the United States (where the concept originated) because of the high level of registration by users. Software authors see benefit in using the method to market software at low cost for a reasonable return. In the UK the level of registration of software is very low compared with the known amount of shareware distributed. Authors therefore feel that the method is unsuccessful. At least two major accounting packages developed in the UK are available via shareware.

Box 4.3 Shareware

any savings to be made by using the system. It is perhaps easier to justify accounting software than other software. The costs of complying with the law are reasonably easy to identify – staff, stationery, audit and accountancy fees, money tied up in creditors' accounts, discounts available on suppliers' accounts, etc. Add to these the more intangible benefits such as better reporting from computer-based systems, and accounting software becomes easy to justify.

Choice of hardware

This is controlled not by the complexity of the software but by the size of the workload as measured by

> number of transactions per day/week/month
> numbers of customers and suppliers
> number of departments and analyses
> how often files are cleared of completed transactions, etc.

It is important that these types of factors are properly estimated before hardware is purchased. Note that many modern microcomputers are perfectly capable of dealing with the accounting requirements of a large proportion of small and medium-sized companies – several hundred invoices per month, up to a thousand customers, etc. However, if your business is specialised or has requirements which impose special loads on the accounting system, ensure that professional advice is obtained before buying even moderate systems.

Choice of software

This is even more important than the choice of hardware. The facilities offered by the software must match the accounting needs of the business. In particular, the software must be flexible enough to grow with a business and be adapted to its needs as the users become more sophisticated in the use of computer-based accounting. Such things as accounting periods, coding structures for customers, expenses, etc., payment terms and credit periods must all be adjustable to suit a specific business. The ability to set these parameters is what marks off sophisticated packages from the simpler ones. Cost is a factor, but the expense of having to start again in a year's time usually outweighs the additional cost of a parameter-driven system. There is one situation in which this advice can be successfully ignored. If the users in a (very) small business are afraid of the impact of computers but recognise the need to do something, it may be worth while introducing a system simpler than otherwise needed in order to build confidence. The simpler menu-driven packages are relatively easy to use because the features built in to the more complex packages are omitted.

If certain organisations require more flexibility than is available in packages, custom-written software is necessary. This is a time-consuming and costly process, but will often give better results in the long run than trying to force a package to work in a situation where it is unsuitable.

The impact of legislation on accounting must also be considered. Because of the number of new laws and regulations which affect accounting practice, keeping accounting systems up to date is a necessary chore. This is done by the suppliers of packages, usually for the payment of a small annual fee. However, if you have custom-written software, you will have to keep it updated yourself – and this can be expensive.

Some accounting packages are extremely powerful for a low price, especially those obtained from shareware sources. Software developers often provide a demonstration disk(s) to enable the prospective user to try out the software to establish its operating characteristics and the type of reports which can be produced before purchasing the package. It is necessary, of course, to assess the features of a package for comparison with those required by the business and assess their degree of correspondence. The cost of the package, to some extent, also depends on whether it is single-user or multi-user, integrated or comprised of several modules.

Some accounting packages require a lengthy installation routine but others are configured very easily by supplying the answer to just a few questions such as the type of printer and monitor installed, whether colour graphics adaptor (CGA), enhanced graphics adaptor (EGA) or video graphics adaptor (VGA), and the disk drive which will be used to copy the software from the distribution disk(s) to a hard disk.

4.4.2 Planning the coding structure

There is a need, when considering the acquisition of accounting software, to look at some design factors which affect the way the system is used. For example, most accounting systems use codes to identify customers, suppliers, expense categories, assets, sales, etc. The flexibility allowed in selecting the type and size of codes is quite crucial in the process of converting from any existing system to a new one. It can be a major task to change the codes an organisation uses – and a significant source of error. Although the staff will eventually get used to new codes, the changeover may be stressful.

Although it sounds simple, many problems can be traced to lack of thought in this area. Codes need to be established before data is entered into a system so that they can be defined to the system before data entry starts. In use, transactions should be coded manually away from the data entry terminal.

Also needed is some thought on how the organisation will be divided up for accounting purposes, and what the layout of standard reports such as profit and loss account, balance sheet and trial balance should be. If a report generator is included as part of the accounting software, then some planning is required before the system is set up to ensure that full benefit of the facility is obtained.

4.4.3 Control in accounting software

A particular feature of accounting packages is the emphasis on control procedures, i.e. ways of ensuring that the package is being used correctly. The aims are to minimise incorrect data entry, whether accidental or deliberate, and to provide facilities to allow the checking of any aspect of the accounts.

The effects of mistakes involving cash or cash value, e.g. invoicing the wrong goods or the wrong value, losing customer account details, producing incorrect financial reports, are particularly serious.

Control procedures can be applied at several levels. The first is to choose tested software from a reliable supplier. Accounting is not the function with which to experiment! Check that the package conforms to established practice and that it is acceptable to your own organisation's accountant. If possible, obtain the views of your external auditors as well.

The next stage is to ensure that the package has good data validation procedures. This means that the package should reject data that is wrong, e.g.

> reject customer codes that do not exist
> reject alphabetic entries in numeric fields
> check that dates are valid, e.g. reject 29/2/89
> check for missing fields

One way to check these sorts of features is to try the package and enter 'silly' data, i.e. data which you know is of the wrong type, e.g. a price of £a.bc. If it accepts some or all of it then be wary.

Controls in accounting systems also cover points such as the following:

- Proper training for staff in the use of the package and in the handling and labelling of disks. A major source of error in accounting systems is the use of the wrong disk during, say, data entry. In particular, the latest data disk must be clearly identified to reduce confusion.
- Unauthorised access to the data on the system must be avoided where possible. If persons not allowed to use a system can be prevented from gaining access, many problems can be avoided. Suitable security measures include password access to the programs, physical access control to the system, division of responsibility for aspects of the system amongst several people.

- Data corruption and error should be avoided by rigorous adherence to backup procedures. Magnetic media are more prone to damage than paper-based systems and multiple copies of all data must be held. Three copies is the minimum that should be kept, with one of them held in separate premises. Note that it is the *data* which is irreplaceable, not the programs (usually).
- Auditing of accounting data *and* procedures is a requirement in most organisations. The system must be developed with the needs of both internal and external auditors in mind. The minimum that is essential is an audit trail which logs every transaction in the order in which it was entered, irrespective of the date of the transaction.

If modules are to be integrated with a nominal ledger it is important to determine the chart of accounts, i.e. the coding structure to be used for the nominal ledger. It provides for grouping various classes of income and expenditure to obtain sub-analyses within the nominal ledger. It facilitates consolidations and enables reports to be more meaningful. Box 4.1 illustrates a typical nominal ledger group description list and indicates the structure of the sub-analysis codes forming the basis of the nominal ledger master file.

4.4.4 User interface

Most packages are menu driven. Some have a hierarchical menu structure (see Figure 4.3), others use drop-down or pop-up menus for the selection of options.

Company menu

Menus provide the means for selecting a specific company accounting system in a multi-company accounting environment. Figure 4.3 illustrates a company menu which includes two companies:

1. Compact Demonstration Company
2. Ron Anderson Limited

When the required company is selected the system menu will then be displayed.

System menu

The system menu lists the different accounting applications from which a selection can be made. The selection of the sales ledger is achieved by typing in 1 at the select number prompt. This then causes the sales ledger program menu to be displayed as shown in Figure 4.3.

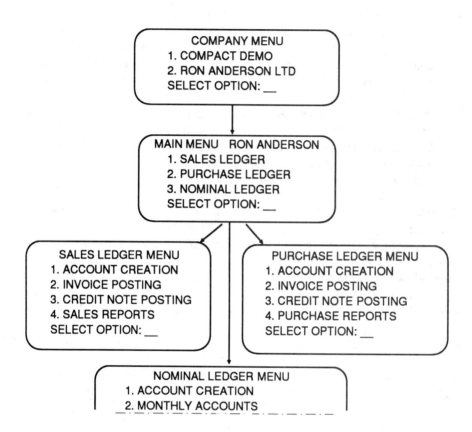

Figure 4.3 Menu structure

Sales ledger program menu

The required option is selected from the program menu. If a new account is being generated it is necessary to select option 1 (Account creation) to create the records required by the accounting system. This is initiated by typing in 1 at the select number prompt. Quite a number of different programs are required for processing the sales ledger.

4.4.5 Implementation

One area which suppliers of software tend to underplay and potential users of accounting software tend to overlook is the difficulty and cost (in time as well as money) of implementing a new accounting system to reflect the current state of the company. Implementation requires several stages, interacting with the current conditions in the company, which cannot be avoided unless the system is a new start when the company is set up. The stages are:

Create and enter lists of customers, suppliers, etc.

Create and enter the chart of accounts.

Select a point in time, say, end of a month or (ideally) end of financial year, at which the new system will start.

Determine from the current system the outstanding balances and unpaid invoices from each sales ledger, purchase ledger and nominal ledger account *at that point in time*.

Enter these details into the system as opening balances.

Start using the system by entering transactions between the selected start point and the present and compare the results with the manual system (*if possible*).

This is the simplest way of implementing an accounting software package in a working company. In practice, it may be considerably more complex. It is probably true that this stage is the most difficult and expensive one in developing a working system.

4.5 REVISION NOTES

1. The accounting function is responsible for the custodianship of a company's assets and for maintaining statutory records.
2. Internal check is a policy which aims at preventing the fraudulent conversion of a company's assets by the separation of duties. Collusion would be necessary between two or more persons to perpetrate a fraud.
3. The management accounting function is responsible for the preparation and distribution of operational and financial information to the various functions. It is also responsible for evaluating capital expenditure projects and the preparation of financial and operating ratios.
4. A cashbook or cashbook software is likely to be used by small retail businesses who trade on a cash basis.
5. Details of a sales accounting system can be analysed to show inputs, outputs and the nature of the files and accounts used in the system.
6. A purchase accounting system provides for the analysis of purchases and services by means of classification codes.
7. Accounting packages are preprepared suites of computer programs for specific applications. Packages are available to suit the needs of all types and size of business.

8. When using computerised accounting systems the double entry aspect of accounting is transparent and is performed automatically by the software. The double entry principle states that every debit should have a corresponding credit, e.g. an invoice value is debited to a customer account and credited to a sales account.
9. Before purchasing an accounting package it should be evaluated to assess if it is compatible with the needs of the business.
10. Some packages are single-user, others have multi-user facilities.
11. Some accounting packages consist of a number of modules which can be used on an integrated basis or as stand-alone modules. A module is designed for a specific application such as the preparation of invoices, for updating a sales ledger or updating stock records.
12. The cost of accounting packages varies; some of them are very expensive, others are not. Very powerful packages can be purchased from shareware sources often at a low price for a quality product.
13. If modules are to be integrated with a nominal ledger a coding structure should be established which is known as a chart of accounts. It provides for grouping various classes of income and expenditure to obtain sub-analyses within the nominal ledger.
14. A system menu lists the different accounting applications from which options can be selected.
15. All modules in an accounting package have similar functions and commands. They also have facilities for creating and maintaining master files, account enquiries and transaction listings, etc.

4.6 SELF-TEST QUESTIONS

1. State the principle of internal check.
2. Define accounting packages and indicate their characteristics.
3. What is meant by the term 'double entry'?
4. What is 'shareware'?
5. What is a 'chart of accounts' and what purpose does it serve?
6. What is a 'system menu'?

4.7 FURTHER READING

1. *Accounting for non-accounting students*, John Dyson, Pitman: London, 1987. A good general introduction.
2. *A Guide to Microcomputer Software for Business*, Anthony Meier, Kogan Page: London, 1988. Refer to chapter 7.
3. *Information Analysis*, Janice Burn and Mike O'Neil, Paradigm / Blackwell Scientific Publications: Oxford, 1987. Refer to chapter 7.
4. *An Introduction to Computer Integrated Business*, L. A. Beddie and S. Raeburn, Prentice Hall International: Hemel Hempstead, 1989. Further details of accounting software are in chapter 2.

Chapter 5

Traditional information processing systems

INTRODUCTION AND SUMMARY

This chapter provides an overview of the nature and characteristics of traditional information processing systems or what may be classed as data processing methods. The chapter includes an outline of the factors which influence the choice of processing system and provides a summary of the stages of the traditional information processing cycle. The terms outlined include batch processing, transaction processing, real-time systems, multi-user and multi-tasking systems. Each of these is used widely for general business information processing. Note that businesses may also use decision support systems, based on spreadsheets, expert systems, executive information systems and databases. These topics are covered in later chapters.

This chapter covers the main elements of a computer system as an introduction to the development of information systems and knowledge-based systems in later chapters. It covers the necessary technical information as well as the principles on which the computer systems you are likely to meet are based. The chapter also looks at centralised versus distributed systems and computer networks.

5.1 THE INFORMATION PROCESSING CYCLE

The processing of data to create information in organisations takes many forms, with firms solving the necessary problems about which data to collect and how to process it in their own way. Divergences and differences in the information cycle may occur depending upon the methods and techniques implemented for specific information systems. The major exception to this is the processing of accounting data, including payroll, where external bodies such as government and the professional accounting institutes lay down statutory and mandatory rules for data handling. However, from this variety a pattern does emerge which is known as the information cycle, with data passing through several stages which are repeated continuously.

Typically the information cycle for the conversion of data into information can be summarised as follows:

COLLECT   data relating to business transactions.
RECORD   data on relevant source documents.
INPUT   data to the processing system or model. The model may be a simulation or spreadsheet model.
TRANSFORM   data into information by appropriate processing operations.
OUTPUT   information in the required format.
INFORM   appropriate recipient by the most suitable means.
MODIFY   the activity or process to which the information relates to attain defined level of performance or specified objectives.

The modified activity or process is then monitored to ensure it is achieving the desired result. This closes the cycle, since monitoring is based on collecting data of the modified system. Compare this description with that of feedback systems in Chapter 3.

5.2 PROCESSING SYSTEMS

Businesses range in size from the small one-man company to medium-sized organisations through to multi-national conglomerates. Each type of business has different information processing needs, e.g. a manufacturing company requires considerably different information from a finance company. Whatever the size and type of business, each needs information produced by an information processing system. The smaller business using a personal computer or the large firm using a central mainframe may process transactions either in batches or individually to suit the circumstances. Applications of a cyclical nature such as the weekly or monthly payroll would be processed in batches because all pay and tax details must be dealt with at the same time for all employees. On the other hand, non-cyclical applications such as the preparation of sales invoices or purchase orders may be processed on an *ad hoc* basis, either several times a day or as and when they become available. The various ways of implementing the stages of the information cycle need to be assessed and the most appropriate method chosen. Factors which need to be considered are shown in Box 5.1. The two broad types of processing systems which are used in organisations are batch processing and transaction processing and these are discussed in the following sections.

Volume	High volumes of data require a fast and powerful processor supported by high speed, high capacity disk drives and fast printers to attain a high throughput rate.
Frequency	The more frequently applications need to be processed the greater is the workload for a given system. This situation would require similar considerations as volume above.
Dispersion	The geographical spread of operating units may necessitate the installation of local or wide area networks to facilitate data interchange between the dispersed operating units. Networks may consist of interconnected workstations, intelligent terminals and small business computers. A local area network is designed to serve a local establishment such as a factory and offices providing a speedy and effective means of communication between them. A wide area network is designed to serve a wide geographical area, perhaps for connecting factories, warehouses and offices in different parts of the country or even different parts of the world.
Power	A centralised computer system may provide economy of scale due to processing all of a business's data centrally. Distributed processing on the other hand provides computing power at any appropriate location at a relatively low cost because of the availability of inexpensive personal computers.
Access	The need for concurrent access to a central computer by many on-line terminals. Such systems need to be able to update files with transaction as they occur. Users may then provide up-to-date information on request or control a critical operation such as airline seat reservation to avoide duplicated booking of seats.

Box 5.1 Processing factors

5.2.1 Batch processing systems

Batch processing is an efficient and cost effective method of dealing with high volume routine transactions relating to such applications as payroll, invoicing and sales accounting, stock control, processing orders, gas and electricity bills and insurance premiums, etc. The method predates computer systems, having been developed early this century to allow processing on large punched card machines. It is still most suitable for large centralised installations where the data arises on a well known and reasonably fixed cycle, such as weekly payroll or monthly accounting periods.

This method processes transactions automatically and all are dealt with at each processing stage before proceeding to the next. Historically, the central computer would be dedicated to a single task, with the data being prepared separately. The file of transaction data, the master files and the program would then be loaded on to the computer and the batch processed in a single operation. The stages are referred to as processing runs, which for most batch processing applications includethe following:

1. Input and validate transaction data.
2. Sort data into the sequence of the master file to be updated.
3. Compute the value of transactions.
4. Update master file.
5. Print output by a printer or display results on a video screen.

This approach has been modified by the availability of more powerful computers, so that data can be prepared for one job whilst a batch from another job is being processed, apparently simultaneously on the one computer. Some of the other features of batch processing are described below.

Key-to-disk system

The traditional technique of processing data in batches requires the encoding of transaction data to magnetic disk by a key-to-disk system. Keyboard operators key in data from transaction documents. The data is collected on magnetic disk and verified before being transferred to the computer centre for processing.

Remote job entry (RJE)

When data requires to be collected from geographically dispersed factories or offices for processing at a centralised centre, a remote job entry (RJE) system is often used. The system transmits data from a pre-encoded disk by communications line to the computer centre where it is stored on disk for subsequent processing in batches.

Batch control

Details of transactions in each batch are recorded on a batch control slip including a batch number, the number of items in the batch, the total value of transactions and any other control totals. A control total may include what is referred to as a hash total, a meaningless total in itself but useful for control purposes, enabling missing or corrupted items to be located when a discrepancy occurs between the control total generated by the computer and that on the control slip. A hash total may consist of the total or transaction reference numbers, such as employee clock numbers, or the total of invoice numbers. Details of batches are recorded in a batch control register.

Master files

Master files relevant to the various applications are updated to show the current status of supplier, customer, stock or employee records, etc. Master files do not change much as each batch is processed, e.g. in a file of customers, most details will stay the same with perhaps a few addresses changing and the outstanding balance figures on most records being amended.

Invalid items report

Errors detected during data validation by the computer are printed out on an invalid items report which indicates the nature of the error. Obvious errors are corrected by the data control section in consultation with the originating department. The processing of valid data usually proceeds without waiting for invalid transactions to be corrected. The batch control totals will need to be amended in such cases. When corrected these will be batched and dealt with the next time the application is due for processing. This depends upon circumstances, however, because it is not feasible to process only a proportion of payroll data – full and complete data must be processed for all employees each pay period. On the other hand invoice transactions with errors can be dealt with when the application is next run. A typical error report relating to the validation of purchase orders is shown in Box 5.2 along with an explanation of the reasons for the errors.

```
Data validation report: Order processing
---- ---------- ------- ----- ----------
Purchase order details
Batch number 10
Date 31/12/92

Item Descr'n    Quan'ty  Error type
---- -------    -------  ----------
123  FOOPUMP         3   Incorrect description
123  FOOTPUMP    92349   Range error
422  BATT CHGR       5   Incorrect item code
     RIM             4   Missing item code
```

Explanation:

The first item has an incorrect description which should read FOOTPUMP. The second item has a range error because the maximum quantity is exceeded. The third item is invalid because the item code does not match the description (in fact the item code is transposed). The last item has a missing item code.

Box 5.2 Sample data validation report

Backup facilities

The security of master files is normally achieved by making a copy of the file, referred to as a backup, either to another disk or to a tape streamer – a device usually used on minicomputers which allows files to be copied at high speed, avoiding the use of expensive disks for this purpose. Backup facilities for transaction files is achieved by retaining the original file and/or making a copy of the file and retaining the original documents.

5.2.2 Transaction processing

One of the major drawbacks of the batch processing approach is the inherent time delays. Data is held until a batch is available, encoded and then held until all the batches can be run on the central computer at a scheduled time. This may be several hours, days, or even weeks after the data arose. During this delay the master files on the computer do not reflect the real state of the business; indeed the real state of the business is unknown. Smaller batches and more frequent runs reduce the time delay and therefore improve the quality of the information held on the computer, helping managers to make better decisions.

The ultimate consequence of reducing batch sizes is batches of one transaction – transaction processing. Data is collected, verified, validated and used to update the master file in a single operation, as soon as possible after the data is generated. Transaction processing poses different problems of data validation in that batch control totals are not meaningful. Therefore some types of error are more likely in a transaction processing system than a batch processing system. Exercising care in systems design can help obviate some of these errors.

Transaction processing systems allow multiple users to run many different programs simultaneously. One could be entering sales invoices, another purchases, another orders, and so on. A multi-access computer is needed for the type of operations outlined to control effectively all the terminals. The computer must have a high capacity internal memory to service many different operations from many different users because it needs to store some software, in the form of the operating system and application programs, for each one. When several terminals have access to the same files as can occur in multi-input high volume processing applications then it is necessary to prevent system clashes. Record locking and unlocking facilities are necessary to prevent a record being accessed by one user when it is being updated by another user until the updating is complete. The record is then unlocked and users can then access the updated version on record.

Real-time system

A transaction processing system can form the basis for a real-time system, so called because the state of the information system is updated as events occur. This type of system is essential in certain circumstances, e.g. for effective stock management when there is a high velocity of stock movements such as occurs in wholesale commodity warehouses supplying supermarkets. If this did not occur excess stocks could build up on the one hand and stock shortages could occur on the other. It is essential to avoid placing replenishment orders when stocks are building up because this would increase storage costs and interest charges on bank loans or overdrafts for financing the excess stock. It is also essential to avoid frequent stock shortages causing customer frustration and possible loss of future orders. Replenishment orders for fast moving items should be placed in sufficient time to avoid stock-out situations – this must take into account the resupply period which is the time which has elapsed from when an order was placed on a supplier to when items were received in the warehouse. This type of system requires to be computer based so that details of stock movements can be keyed in by an operator sitting at a keyboard connected to a computer – this is referred to as on-line transaction processing. The same type of system is needed for a building society, bank or airline reservation system as it is essential to update records in files so that the information they contain represents the current status of the physical system. In the case of an airline, a real-time seat reservation system attempts to avoid double booking of aircraft seats on a particular flight, to a particular destination on a specific day. Real-time banking and building society operations record transactions as they occur so that the current status of account balances is always known. This prevents customers overdrawing and provides financial data for management purposes.

5.3 COMPUTER SYSTEMS

Computer systems consist of three principal elements – hardware, software and data. This section covers the first two of these, with the major topic being the software. This is because hardware is usually an accessory in a computer system and the hardware without the software is not useful. It is actually the software which allows the user to solve problems and run applications. The hardware provides the basic environment for software and executes instructions, but these instructions are defined and controlled by the software.

5.3.1 Hardware

Hardware is the most visible part of computing, the parts which can be touched. It is all the computer machinery in High Street stores or in computer installations. That is, plastic or metal cabinets, various types of display screens, a few flashing console lights, etc, all making subdued clicking and whirring noises when working.

More important than what the machinery looks like is what it does. Any computer user needs to understand the functions and interactions of these pieces of equipment, to move one step away from the black box principle. At its simplest, a computer has four functional components. Figure 5.1 displays a functional model of the hardware components of the computer, with the interaction and data flow between the components shown by the arrows. Box 5.3 explains each component in more detail. Box 5.4 specifies how data storage is measured, a cause of confusion to new computer users.

Remember, this is a functional, or logical, picture. In reality, each functional component can have several different appearances. There may be one or more actual pieces of equipment comprising each functional component. In the case of the central part they are called processors; in the case of the other three components they are called peripherals. It is the business or organisation which decides on just how many and just what type of peripherals are needed to comprise each of the four functional components. This decision is taken in the light of organisational policy and requirements. Thus, each organisation will have its own particular and specific computer configuration, i.e. a working composition of processors and peripherals. (The actual number of peripherals in a configuration will also vary according to the size and capacity of the

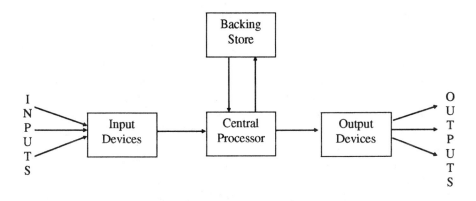

Figure 5.1 Hardware components of a computer

INPUT DEVICES can be used in two ways. Firstly, during data entry they allow large volumes of data to be input to the computer, prior to storage or use in calculations. Secondly, and more importantly for the business user, they are the medium through which commands, say, to run a program or print a report. This dialogue is maintained by means of menus, icons or commands, depending on the way in which the system has been designed.

OUTPUT DEVICES can also be used in two ways. Firstly, as a way of responding to user dialogue. The second way is the more familiar one of presenting the results of calculations or other computer processes in a manner and on a medium suitable to the user. The manner can be by words, tables or graphics (diagrams) or by a mixture of the three.

BACKING STORE (or SECONDARY MEMORY) stores very large quantities of data in a format for long-term storage. The storage is *non-volatile*, i.e. the data remains intact and valid even when the computer is not connected to the power supply. Thus, a user may make reference to the data on backing store in the production reports and enquiries. Application programs and other items of software are also held on backing store.

The CENTRAL PROCESSOR comprises two separate parts, the central processing unit (CPU) and the main memory. The CPU carries out the arithmetic and logical processes to which data is subjected and exercises control over the other components. Main or primary memory provides very fast access to data but usually has a much smaller capacity than backing store. In addition, the data is *volatile*, i.e. lost when the power is removed.

Box 5.3 Hardware elements defined

processor.) Examples of peripherals can be found in any textbook on computer systems (see Section 5.7).

Further, a particular type of peripheral may operate under the guise of one or more of the functional components. In one organisation, personnel details of all employees may be held on floppy disks, which are thus functioning as backing store. In another company, the floppy disk may be used to capture data on rental payments by customers at local branches and then sent to Head Office for the data to be transferred to the accounts. The floppy disk is then functioning both as an input component and as an output component. This begins to sound complicated, but it also underlines the versatility of much of the hardware.

Computer processors come in four basic sizes, namely microcomputers, minicomputers, mainframes and supercomputers in increasing order of size. The most common of these is the microcomputer, a small computer system based around an electronic device called a microprocessor. This is a chip made by a specialist company and installed in computers made by many different manufacturers, giving the economies of scale which lead to the very low price of microcomputers. Box 5.5 explains something of the types of microprocessor available.

In larger computer systems (minicomputers, mainframes and super-

What you need to know about internal computer storage is actually quite simple. Computers are binary devices. This means that the workings of the machine recognise two states, represented by 0 and 1 (equivalent to OFF and ON in a switch). These two numbers are called 'bits' and all data is represented by groups of bits. In modern computers, the standard group is based on 8 bits, universally called a 'byte'.

Storage in computer systems tends to be measured in bytes or multiples of bytes. For various reasons, these multiples tend to be slightly different from the hundreds, thousands, millions that we are used to dealing with in decimal arithmetic. The principle is the same as with decimal but Greek names are used to give a scientific air to the terminology. Thus

one kilobyte (kb) = 1024 bytes
one megabyte (Mb) = 1024 kilobytes
one gigabyte (Gb) = 1024 megabytes
one terabyte (Tb) = 1024 gigabytes

The first two of these are in common usage, the last two are not. However, due to the falling costs of computer storage and the increasing size of systems, gigabyte storage systems are not uncommon and terabyte systems will be available in the foreseeable future.

Box 5.4 Data in computer storage

computers), the processor is always proprietary, i.e. will be designed and installed only in that computer by a single manufacturer. Historically, mainframe computers came first, in the 1950s, and formed the basis of organisational computing for many years, with IBM as the major manufacturer. In the late 1960s, a smaller range of computers was developed by competitors of IBM to meet specific needs. These were called minicomputers. Super-computers were a development of the 1970s, to meet the needs of the scientific community for very powerful and fast 'number-crunchers' to process the results of experiments. They are now also used for weather forecasting, geological work, oil and metal prospecting, nuclear physics, graphical simulations (including for the film industry), virtual reality and other tasks which require billions of calculations in the shortest possible time.

5.3.2 Software

Software is the general term for instructions which command the computer hardware and, in some cases, the other software. These instructions are written in a programming language and set down as statements, to be read and executed one at a time in sequence. They read rather like a recipe – step 1, then step 2,

The microprocessor is (in some ways) the equivalent of the engine in a car. It is the microprocessor which provides the 'power' to process data and execute programs. In rather the same way as the number of cylinders in a car gives a (very) crude guide to the power of a car, the microprocessor has a quotable number which gives a guide to the power of the microcomputer. It is not the only factor, or even the most important one, but it is easy to define. The factor in question is the number of bits of data which the processor can deal with in an instruction and the values in typical microprocessors are:

8 bit   now becoming obsolete, but still found in a proportion of existing microcomputers.

16 bit   the standard of the late 1980s and probably still (in 1992) the most commonly used size.

32 bit   the high performance microprocessor and undoubtedly the standard of the 1990s.

In general, 16 bit microprocessors are more powerful than 8 bit ones, and 32 bit ones are more powerful than 16 bit ones. Be warned, however, that software and other factors can more than blur the distinctions between each class. Note also that you cannot 'count' the bits by looking at the microprocessor – you have to find out from a data sheet what the number of bits is. (Larger computers can also be measured in this way, although it is quite unusual. It is actually quite difficult to measure the 'power' of a computer and certainly well beyond the scope of this book.)

     There are two major manufacturers of microprocessors, Intel and Motorola, both American companies. Intel design and produce the microprocessors used in IBM PCs and compatible microcomputers. Intel devices are numbered 8086, 80286, 80386, 80486, leading to the generic reference 80x86 meaning any Intel chip in this series. Often the leading 80 is dropped and PCs are referred to as 286s, 386s, etc., depending on the microprocessor fitted.

     Motorola microprocessors are fitted to Apple Macintosh microcomputers and are numbered in a series based on 68000, although it is not usual to quote the processor version in the same way as for PCs.

     Note that these two major types of microprocessors are completely incompatible in software terms and programs and operating systems cannot easily be swapped between PCs and Macintoshs.

Box 5.5 Types of microprocessor

etc. This text does not cover programming. What is important is to recognise and comprehend that there is not one single item of software, but several items interacting with one another. The major items of software can be pictured as being arranged in layers around the hardware, as in Figure 5.2. The figure does not show every possible type of software. Rather, for clarity, it is confined to the most common types used on microcomputers.

     The purpose of each of these pieces of software is to instruct the hardware

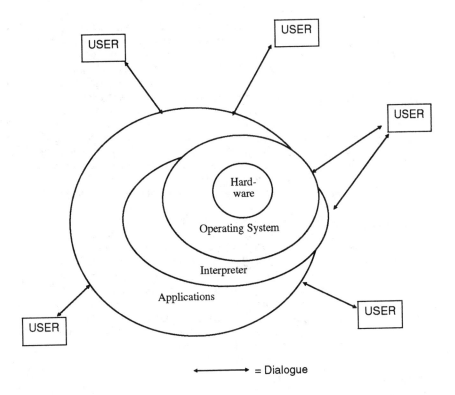

Figure 5.2 Software layers

to perform some task (e.g. add three numbers, accept new stock price from the keyboard, print employee name). However, the only software to command the hardware directly is the one which is closest to it, the operating system (OS). Any other has to interact with the software between it and the hardware.

The user dialogue is always directly with the outermost software layer. A closer look at the diagram will show that, in some cases, this means the operating system itself (see the arrow at the top right), whilst in others it means being three layers removed. The reason for this is that each layer of software builds on the previous one in some manner. A rule of thumb would be that, the more layers of software between the user and the operating system, the more English-like and friendly the user dialogue will become. Box 5.6 outlines the features of the types of dialogue common on business computers. Perhaps voice-driven computers may be available in the near future, but for the moment the dialogue will be via keyboards and screen.

COMMAND-DRIVEN. With this type of interface, the user is presented with a prompt and expected to type the exact command needed to invoke the process required. A command could be two characters, or something closer to a sentence, in order to specify precisely what is needed. In addition, the command will use abbreviations of some sort and have a well defined syntax and structure which may make it look very complex to a novice user.

MENU-DRIVEN. A menu is a set of options presented on screen. You simply select one of the options to carry out the process you wish. Menus certainly save your fingers, because a single keystroke will begin the next process. The number of options on a menu is virtually limitless, but because of screen size and complexity, it is generally no more than a dozen. However, it may require more than one menu screen to define precisely what you want to do. To this end, where there are a number of menus, then the first one you meet will show pretty general options, and subsequent ones will refine the choice.

An extension of the menu concept is the graphical user interface, a concept which involves windows and icons to offer choice, rather than text fields. Whatever the method of choice, menus are shorthand versions of commands insofar as the number of keystrokes is concerned. They are also easier to follow and to get out of if you make a mistake. The command is a shorthand form of the menu though, as far as time is concerned, when the number of menus needed to carry out the same process is large, it can be very annoying to select an option from five menus regularly, because it takes time for the screen to refresh and display the next menu. The one-line command can seem very welcoming to an experienced user.

Box 5.6 Types of user dialogue

5.3.3 Operating system

The operating system is software which allows the user to control the various parts of a computer system and controls the transmission of data between the functional components, e.g. from backing store disk to output printer via main memory, or from disk to main memory and back to disk. It is the single most important piece of software and it creates the environment for running other programs on the computer. With multi-user systems, the operating system tasks of scheduling jobs and making the most efficient use of the resources of the computer are essential. The simplest computers are capable of carrying out input, processing or output operations in succession for each unit of data. Slightly more sophisticated ones are able to overlap some of these operations to a certain extent, and this process is known as simultaneity. For example, a print program uses a lot of output time but little CPU time (unless it performs very complex calculations and manipulations on the data prior to printing). On the other hand, a program which calculates something based on many values and rules will be heavy on CPU usage.

CONTROL OF MULTI-TASKING – allowing several programs to run apparently simultaneously for each user. This utilises the fact that all programs are different in the way in which they use the computer resources. Some programs use a great deal of peripheral time (often referred to as 'peripheral-bound') whereas others take up more CPU time but very little input–output time (referred to as 'CPU-bound').

COMMUNICATIONS – control of the data transmissions between a computer and its peripherals and between two or more computers.

SPOOLING – a simple but clever method of making efficient use of peripherals. The word 'spool' comes from Simultaneous Printing Operations On-Line and is used to help avoid the (in computer terms) extreme slowness of printing. The OS sends any output intended for the printer to a disk file instead of directly to the printer. This shortens the run time of the program as the disk is a much faster device than the printer. The OS transfers the output from the disk to the printer when the printer is free, and means that the printing may continue after the program is finished. This later print is faster because it is a simple task to copy records from disk to printer.

SOFTWARE CONTROL – of all the other application software so that it is available when needed.

LOGGING – of all jobs run, their time and date of start and completion and any which failed to complete. This is needed for system security and auditing.

PRIORITIES – in a large system jobs are given a priority rating either by the staff who manage the system or by the OS itself. An example of this is clear from the 'foreground' and 'background' modes of working. These terms refer to the areas of memory in which the program is run. Programs with a low priority rating can be run in the background whilst the higher priority jobs run in the foreground, and this is especially true when the background jobs require no interaction with the user (e.g. a print spooling) but the foreground jobs require user interaction (e.g. a file enquiry, order entry). High priority jobs get first call on the machine resources and hence run quickly; the low priority ones get what is left and therefore run more slowly.

CONCURRENCY – software has to be careful not to let transaction data be lost. Concurrency occurs when two or more processes want to update the same data at the same point in time. To permit this to happen in an uncontrolled manner leads to loss of data and unpredictable results. Therefore, the OS takes control and ensures that the integrity of the data and the system remains intact.

Box 5.7 Functions of an operating system

The OS is the innermost piece of software as shown in Figure 5.2. It has a wide range of functions, although those of a stand-alone microcomputer will be less numerous than those of a large mainframe. The more complex the configuration, the more complex the operating system needs to be. The OS is in fact a suite of programs, and one of them, the executive, will remain resident in main memory whilst the computer is switched on. The executive controls all the other programs in the suite as well as the application programs. The main functions of an operating system are summarised in Box 5.7.

Once upon a time there was little choice in the matter of which operating system arrived when a computer was acquired. The proprietary operating system which 'fitted' the model of computer purchased was supplied (a bit like engines in cars really). Nowadays this is mostly untrue and there will be a number of operating systems compatible with the computer you wish to buy. In the case of microcomputers, market forces have now reduced the competition to only two

---

The operating system called Unix was originally developed in Bell Telephone Laboratories in the USA purely for use in research and related areas (like academic institutions) on Digital Equipment Company (DEC) minicomputers. It is now available in many versions on many computers. As well as all the usual OS functions, Unix has a wide range of facilities, many non-existent in other operating systems, which are designed to save the user from having to write the appropriate program code to carry out common tasks. For example, searching for a particular string of characters in a file usually requires a program to be written in a high level language. Unix offers a simple command to carry out this type of task.

Unix is the subject of extreme emotions – fanatical loyalty or hatred – and most people who have come across it fall into one of these camps. The reason for this principally comes from the syntax of the commands, or the user dialogue. It is terse, distinctly un-English-like, and probably ungrammatical too. Most systems programmers and computer professionals love it; other users are not enamoured of it.

Here are a few typical Unix commands.

```
grep -v cat stock
```

means 'print on the screen all the records in a file with the filename "stock" which contain the string of characters "cat"'.

```
pwd
```

means 'print name of the directory (an area of disc) in which you are working'.

However, it is a rich OS in terms of its facilities, and complex for the same reasons. There are several software packages which fit on top of Unix – languages, graphics manipulation packages, database management systems – and the number is growing as Unix becomes more commercially acceptable.

Box 5.8 Unix

or three contenders. There are a few standards in this field, operating systems which have stood the test of time and proved beneficial to a particular type of user in a particular environment. Examples include Unix, MS-DOS and Pick, each of which is explained below, either in Boxes 5.8 and 5.9 or in the text.

It is a case of horses for courses and, apart from the solid fact that at least

---

The Pick operating system was named after a certain Richard Pick, who sought to develop an OS which allowed users of all grades of sophistication to use it for file and data manipulation. Thus it supports a single type of file – one which has a unique key for every record – and where records in the same file, whilst having the same format, need not be of the same length. The advantage of this variable-length record approach comes with the storage of quantities of text fields, the contents of which are highly variable in the number of characters used. It is economical in disk space, because, otherwise, all fields are adjudged to be of maximum length. Most records can be given a unique key value, even if it is not inherent in the data, simply by allocating a sequential code to it.

The OS file and data manipulation facilities are second to none. The commands are an approximation to English, and support retrieval and update of selected records. Moreover, PICK permits the selection of particular record occurrences based on the value of ANY of the fields in the record. (Naturally, the key field is assumed to be the most frequent selector and makes for the fastest retrieval time.)

The following are typical Pick commands to retrieve and amend records in a stock control situation.

```
list stock with QOH > 5000
```

means 'find all records where the quantity-on-hand is greater than 5000 units'.

```
list stock with description = 'plug' and with no QOH
```

means 'list records of plugs with no entry in QOH field'.

High level language programming is also supported, typically through BASIC. There are additional facilities to store OS commands in a file. This is useful if some manipulation commands are used frequently, as you can simply call up the file rather than retype the commands each time. Pick is for standard data processing functions, where not all the processing is to be performed by COBOL programs, and where a user may generate his or her own management information system from the files of the operational system.

It is asserted that any user can design and implement an application system from scratch without recourse to writing programs. This is true but, in the experience of the authors, it takes a lot of time, reading of manuals, and understanding of Pick to come up with a system which is acceptable both visually and in terms of processing consistency and integrity. Perseverance brings its own rewards though!

Box 5.9 The Pick operating system

one OS is required, the only guidance that can be given is to note the type of environment in which each one thrives and the types of application for which it is used. Criteria which should be borne in mind in the selection of an operating system are the range of application software available for it, the style of dialogue and file handling facilities.

The brief overview given of the more popular, or standard, OS currently available is not intended to imply that only those mentioned should be considered. There are other ones around and the need and environment of the computer system must be considered. However, the principal advantage of using a popular OS is that there is a large user base (to go to for advice and help) and a plethora of application software. The OS acquired must have facilities to match the needs of the application(s). Gather information from other users and a sympathetic computer professional on the matter, although the final judgement can only be made by those directly involved.

One further point to note. The documentation for any operating system is complex. The manuals at first glance will appear to be in a foreign language and will take some studying. Do not avoid the confrontation; take comfort from the fact that day-to-day running of a computer only uses a small portion of the utilities, and the manual is ready as a reference when the need arises.

Microcomputer operating systems

There are effectively only two standard operating systems in use in microcomputers, MS-DOS from Microsoft Inc. and the Apple Macintosh OS. Many different operating systems exist on mainframe computers and minicomputers, including several from the same manufacturer. The only operating system which is available for computers of all sizes is Unix.

MS-DOS runs on microcomputers of all sizes which use a microprocessor from the 80x86 series and is a generalised version of PC-DOS, the IBM PC operating system also written by Microsoft. It is command line driven, very powerful, but thought not very user-friendly for casual and inexperienced users. It is guaranteed that you will never be short of choice of application software of all varieties if you use MS-DOS as there are literally thousands of packages and programs designed to run under this OS. There are a few minor competitors to MS-DOS, the principal of which being DR-DOS from Digital Research Inc. Most are compatible with MS-DOS (in order that their users are able to run the software available for MS-DOS) but try to offer a few extra features. If these are useful, they tend to appear in MS-DOS soon thereafter, so that new versions of all have to be produced.

The Apple Macintosh operating system is designed, as the name suggests, only for a specific make of microcomputer, the Apple Macintosh. This computer uses the 68000 series of microprocessors, a different chip from the PC range.

This OS is menu-driven but uses a graphics menu as well as text ones and a pointing device to select options. The approach was first developed in the early 1980s by Rank Xerox at one of their research establishments and pioneered as its main operating system by Apple. This type of OS is now known as a graphical user interface (GUI) and is thought to be particularly suitable for casual and inexperienced users (see Box 5.6 on dialogues).

Graphical user interfaces are available for PCs (see Box 5.10) and these are becoming very popular, although at least an 80386 processor and 2 Mb of memory is required to make full use of the facilities offered. GUI software displays images on the video screen and provides DOS and other operating systems with a friendly interface, avoiding the need for the computer operator to use OS commands. To run a program using a GUI, it is only necessary to point to the appropriate program name with the mouse and click. A window is then opened for the selected application.

Graphical user interface (GUI) software provides users with a graphical display when the computer is switched on. Such an interface or front-end makes the system more user-friendly. The display consists of *icons*, small symbols representing files or activities. Each icon represents an option and is selected by a *point and pick* technique using a *pointer* on screen controlled by a *mouse*. A mouse is a small hand-held electromechanical device which can be moved in any direction across the desk surface. A pointer is a symbol which indicates a location on the screen. The pointer moves as the mouse moves in terms of direction and distance. Thus a user can point to any one of various items on a screen. Selection of an option on a screen display is by means of clicking a button, of which a mouse typically has two or three. This avoids the need to use OS commands.

Often the display is split into several areas, each of which can contain several icons. Each area is called a *window* and can run a separate task. Windows may overlap. This is the basis of what is referred to as 'windows' software, several examples of which are mentioned below.

Microsoft Windows 3.1 acts as a front-end to MS-DOS for PCs with an 80286, 80386 or 80486 processor. The faster the machine the better the performance.

IBM's *Presentation Manager* is the GUI for microcomputers which have OS/2 as the operating system.

The DEC *NewWave* windows desktop environment has a common user interface for diverse operating systems and applications providing a unified framework for enterprise-wide computing.

X-Windows is a cross-platform graphical interface that will allow a program run on a Unix system to display its output and receive its input on an IBM PC or an Apple Macintosh, for instance, forming a link between DOS- and Unix-based machines.

Box 5.10 Graphical user interface software

5.3.4 Multi-tasking

Multi-tasking is a technique which allows two or more programs to run apparently simultaneously on a single computer. A fast processor is required because the computer has to switch between programs at high speed. Each program is allocated a portion of processing time known as a 'time slice', giving the impression that more than one task is being processed at the same time. This is not so, however: only one task is performed at any one moment but because the processor is switching from one task to the other at high speed it gives the impression of processing more than one task at a time.

The technique can increase processing productivity if more applications are processed in a shorter time than would be the case if they were processed sequentially. This occurs if each program has to wait for a relatively slow peripheral such as a printer. Since the computer can be a million times faster than a peripheral, even the short delay waiting for a character to be printed or a key to be pressed could process many instructions. So if the computer can transfer to another program, it can execute some of its instructions and then come back to the original program. It is important to appreciate, however, that the elapsed time for each separate task will be increased.

Originally developed for large mainframe computers in the 1960s and 1970s, multi-tasking is now possible on powerful PCs. In particular, GUI software allows a different task to be opened in each window and allows text and data to be transferred from one task to another. This process is sometimes referred to as dynamic data exchange (DDE).

5.4 CENTRALISED AND DISTRIBUTED COMPUTING

Computer power in a large business prior to the inception of small business computers, local and wide area networks and on-line terminal base operations was provided by a centralised mainframe computer. The mainframe installation processed the transactions relating to each of the business functions including those of the payroll department, accounts office, production planning and stock control, which were channelled to the central computer functioning as the central hub of a business's information systems. This was also applicable to businesses with geographically dispersed operating units consisting of branch works, warehouses and offices. The applications were wide and varied depending upon the nature of a specific business. Batch processing was used to process large volumes of data on a three-shift basis enabling the computer to be kept fully occupied. This was an economic necessity because of the high cost of the investment in hardware, software, systems development and the cost of operating the system.

Due to the current, relatively low cost of small computers and the diversity and geographical dispersion of operations in some businesses, distributed processing facilities are found to be more appropriate. Distributed processing provides computing power to any business location or function wherever it serves a useful purpose. Information processing then becomes a localised rather than a centralised activity allowing autonomous control of such activities. Even with distributed processing it is necessary to conduct operations within the framework of corporate policy. This necessitates an adherence to information processing standards and a high degree of coordination between Head Office and dispersed factories and other operating units to accord to corporate requirements. Autonomy of this type provides the foundation to pursue common aims but without undue influence from central management.

5.4.1 Multi-user systems

The purpose of any information system is to provide an efficient means of processing business transactions by connecting terminals to a computer. Multi-terminal operations are controlled by a centrally located mainframe or mini-computer. The terminals are connected by communication lines enabling the various departments of a business to use computing facilities on a multi-user basis, i.e. many users can simultaneously use the processing power of the central computer. The processing tasks performed by each terminal depend on the nature of the functional activities. One terminal may be used for product enquiries when the operator is in contact with customers on the telephone or in direct contact with them in a gas or electricity show room, for instance. In other functions terminals could be used for payroll processing, account enquiries and updating and for building business models using spreadsheets. Terminals are used in many different types of business: in airlines to obtain information relating to the availability of seats on specific flights on stated dates; banking enquiry systems to check the status of customers' accounts; enquiries from travel agents to tour operators for holiday enquiries; and so on.

Figure 5.3 shows the elements of a typical multi-user system. The example is based on a manufacturing or warehouse-based business but the principles apply to all systems of this type. Almost all large computer systems in business use are multi-user, as are many based on microcomputers. Note that this is not the only way to build a multi-user system; local area networks (see Section 5.4.2) also provide such facilities.

Type of communication line

The number and location of terminals will have a bearing on the number and type of communication line required. If terminals are located within, say, 4000 feet of a computer, then internal cables can be used but if the terminals are geographically dispersed, perhaps in branch sales offices, then leased private telephone lines will be necessary in order to obtain exclusive use of them whenever they are needed. If the public telephone lines are used delays are likely to occur due to lines being engaged when required.

Cluster controller

Cluster controllers may be installed in multi-terminal locations so that communication lines can be shared rather than having one line allocated to each terminal which would be expensive. Communication lines may be connected to a multiplexer, communications processor or front-end processor. A multiplexer is a device which batches signals from several terminals transmitting on slow

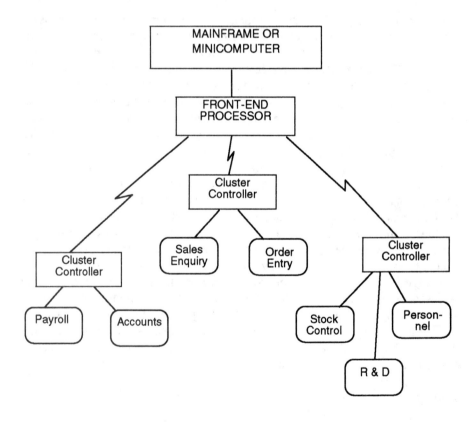

Figure 5.3 Elements of a multi-user system

speed lines. It accommodates a number of channels on a single high speed line enabling signals to be received at high speed by the computer.

Front-end processor

A front-end processor supports the operations of a mainframe by performing tasks which it would otherwise need to do itself which would increase the overall time spent on computing activities. This would occur in instances when the mainframe had to switch from its current task to perform code conversions, editing, data validation, terminal recognition and control of the communication lines.

5.4.2 Local area networks (LANs)

Local area networks link a number of workstations, terminals and personal computers via a communication network. Each device connected to the network is known as a node. Transactions are processed by each of the nodes according to their specific needs. Networks also provide facilities for transmitting data between nodes and to a corporate mainframe for the interchange of information and for accessing a database. The speed of transmission varies between 1 and 12 million bits per second which is much faster than the speed of telephone lines. A variety of devices and facilities are required to enable networks to function. These include:

1. A communication server for linking network users to a variety of communication devices by telephone line connections.
2. A print server linking each network user with high speed printing facilities.

3. A file server for controlling the storage of documents, programs and data files on high capacity disks.

Local area networks are used to provide users with some of the advantages of large mainframe-based systems along with the flexibility and ease of use of personal computers. Whereas other networks are seen as ways of giving a personal computer access to a wide range of services on an *ad hoc* basis, a LAN is often seen as a computer system in its own right. It is a single system which offers a range of facilities on a permanent basis.

The facilities provided by a typical LAN include:

- electronic mail
- peripheral sharing

- data sharing, including file transfer
- office automation
- industrial control
- distributed computing.

Of these, the first three are by far the most common, but new applications which make use of the other facilities are constantly being developed.

LANs typically allow users to use any software which can be used on a stand-alone personal computer. In particular, any form of screen display and user dialogue is permitted, subject only to the type of micro-computer in use. Thus windows, mice, icons, menus are all permitted and the speeds of transmission of data are high, perhaps hundreds of thousands of characters per second. Software may be stored anywhere on the system and loaded into the memory of a user's computer via the network, avoiding the use of floppy disks. It is these sorts of characteristics which enable a user to see a LAN as a single system – it behaves like a single, large, powerful machine.

Network topologies

There are many different ways of building a network from the same basic components, i.e. computers and their communication links. The 'topology' of a network is the logical 'shape' or pattern of interconnection of the various components and is usually named after the outline the network creates when drawn on paper. The full meaning of this will become apparent below when each of the common types is covered. Needless to say, networks look nothing like their names when actually installed in an office or other building.

Transmission of data over a network is by one of two basic methods – 'point-to-point' or 'broadcast'. Point-to-point, as the name suggests, means that messages sent out from one point on the network travel by a direct link to another point. Perhaps the most common example of this type of network is the 'star' in which many terminals are each connected to a central node, usually a minicomputer or a mainframe (see Figure 5.3).

The broadcast method does not utilise direct links between nodes. Instead, a common link is used to which all nodes are connected. Messages between nodes are sent on the common link to all other nodes; only the node(s) to which the message is addressed actually bother to pick up the message. The basic broadcast topology is the 'bus'.

5.4.3 Wide area networks (WANs)

A wide area network is a geographically dispersed set of computers which can be connected together, either permanently or as required. The users of a WAN may all be members of the same organisation or, more usually, independent of each other. The WAN is normally set up and operated by a specialist company, e.g. a company such as BT, and the operator's choice dictates the nature of the network. The most common use of a WAN is as a transmission medium for value-added network services (VANS). The WAN is used because of the services it provides access to, not merely for computer-to-computer communication.

A WAN is generally so large as to defy categorisation in terms of its 'shape' (compare network topologies in Section 5.3.2). Some are a bit like Topsy in having 'just growed', others were planned to meet a particular need. A nationwide network is probably best thought of as a mesh, with multiple possible routes through many nodes and communication links. This ensures that, in the event of a node or a link being inoperative, another route for messages is possible. Nationwide networks are used by BT to provide the Telecom Gold service and by banks and building societies to provide links to their ATMs – the now ubiquitous 'hole-in-the-wall' cash dispensers.

WANs developed from the 'timesharing' computer systems which were popular in the 1960s and 70s. Those systems offered access to computer processing power. Modern WANs offer a much wider range of services, including teleshopping, home and office banking, database access, rail and theatre booking, airline flight details worldwide, company searches and so on, although electronic mail is probably the primary service. Many multi-national companies use electronic mail to keep in touch with branches around the world daily, allowing Head Office greater control than before. Thus communication rather than processing is the motivating factor in the use of such systems.

5.4.4 Gateways

The existence of many networks, some LANs, some WANs, some single site, some organisation wide, some national, some international, some dedicated to particular services or groups of users, some open to anyone who cares to pay, leads naturally to the situation where users will need to access more than one network. There are two basic ways of approaching this problem – either the user becomes a member of each network he or she requires to access or links are established between networks to allow messages and services to pass from one to the other. The second approach has many advantages, not the least of which is that the user only has fewer sets of access codes to remember, and these internetwork links are now generally called 'gateways'.

A gateway is more than just a few pieces of wire linking each network. It is generally a dedicated computer system which performs the necessary signal and data conversions necessary for a message to be acceptable to the receiving networks. It is not enough merely to interconnect the computers physically; conversion processes at data levels are necessary to ensure that a message is properly transmitted. Gateways mean that it is now possible to send and receive telexes from most WANs, such as Telecom Gold. A computer with a special telex number is the link between the old and the new systems. Users of a UK WAN can send messages to many users in other countries which have a compatible network. Gateways are now being provided between WANs operated by different companies, such as Telecom Gold and Mercurylink.

5.5 REVISION NOTES

1. Each type of business has different processing needs.
2. High volume data processing requirements need a fast and powerful processor and high speed peripherals. The term peripheral relates to the input, output and storage devices connected to the computer by cables. These include keyboards, disk drives and printers.
3. The geographical dispersion of operating units may necessitate the installation of local or wide area networks.
4. A centralised computer system may provide economy of scale due to processing all data centrally.
5. Distributed processing provides computing power wherever it serves a useful purpose in the organisation.
6. Real-time systems respond to events as they occur ensuring that the stored information represents the status of the real-world system.
7. Batch processing is an efficient and cost effective method of processing large volumes of routine transaction data in batches.
8. Batches of transactions are controlled throughout all stages of processing by a batch control slip and the data control section to ensure that all data received from user departments is actually processed. The term 'user department' means the department originating the transaction data for whom processing is carried out.
9. The term master file is used to describe a set of records relating to a specific application such as payroll or stock control which are stored on magnetic media. The records in the files are updated with transaction data and amendments to ensure they represent their current status.
10. Errors detected during a data validation routine are either displayed on the screen or printed out on an invalid items report.
11. File security is normally achieved by making a copy of the master file which is referred to as 'backup'. Security is required as a precautionary measure to offset the effects on the business of losing its information stored

in the files. This may occur if a file is stolen, corrupted during processing by overwriting or accidentally wiped clean causing all its contents to be lost.

12. Instead of processing transactions in batches some applications process individual transactions as they occur; this is referred to as transaction processing.

13. Multi-user applications allow several users to share processor time for their own processing requirements. Each user is connected to the processor by a terminal.

14. Multi-tasking is a technique which allows two or more programs to run simultaneously. This technique is sometimes referred to as multi-programming.

15. GUI is an abbreviation for Graphical User Interface, software which provides users with a graphical display when the computer is switched on and which makes the system more user-friendly.

16. A mouse can be used to position a pointer at any location on the screen. Thus a user can point to any one of various items on a screen. Selection of an option on a screen display is by means of clicking one of the mouse's buttons.

5.6 SELF-TEST QUESTIONS

1. Why do high volume data processing systems need a fast, powerful processor and high speed peripherals?
2. What is a 'peripheral'?
3. Distinguish between centralised and distributed processing.
4. What is the nature of real-time systems?
5. In what way are batches of transactions controlled?
6. What is a master file?
7. What is the purpose of data validation?
8. Explain why backup files are essential in a business computer system.
9. Distinguish between the terms 'multi-user' and 'multi-tasking'.
10. Define the term 'GUI' and state its purpose.
11. Define EACH of the terms: icon, point and pick, cursor, and mouse.

5.7 FURTHER READING

1. *Computer Studies – A First Year Course*, Ron Anderson, Blackwell Scientific Publications: Oxford, 1990. Refer to chapter 10.

2. *Data Processing, Volume 1 Principles and Practice*, 7th edn, M. & E. Handbooks/Pitman: London, 1990. Refer to chapters 1, 2, 13—15.
3. *Business Data Systems*, 4th edn, H. D. Clifton, Prentice Hall International: Hemel Hempstead, 1990. Refer to chapter 2.
4. *An Introduction to Computer Integrated Business*, L. A. Beddie and S. Raeburn, Prentice Hall International: Hemel Hempstead, 1989. Further details of networks and computer communications are in chapter 8.

Chapter 6

The development of information systems

INTRODUCTION AND SUMMARY

This chapter outlines the approach to the development of information systems commencing with a definition of engineering and systems engineering. The chapter continues by discussing the human aspects of systems development and particularly the need to co-opt the services of personnel in the departments affected. An overview is then provided of the stages of system development. Structured systems analysis methodologies are then discussed, with an overview of Structured Systems Analysis and Design Method (SSADM) and the Yourdon Structured Method (YSM).

6.1 ENGINEERING

Engineering may be defined as the application of scientific principles to the analysis, design, construction and operation of machines, business systems and other structures. The definition is very relevant to the design and construction of information systems which are structures developed by the application of scientific principles of analysis prior to engineering a more effective physical system.

Systems engineering is the modern term used to describe the whole of the systems development life cycle, and usually, to the application of structured analysis and design methodologies and the use of software engineering techniques and tools for the development of information systems. Systems engineering takes into account various views of design problems and solves them from a business and organisational perspective. Systems engineering takes all viewpoints into consideration in the development of the optimum system, i.e. the system which optimises the performance of a particular function of the business or the activities of the business as a whole. Software engineering often utilises CASE tools for the development of systems, and these are the subject of Chapter 8.

6.2 HUMAN ASPECTS OF SYSTEMS DEVELOPMENT

The human aspects of systems development are sometimes forgotten in the rush to create new systems. The engineering aspects are interesting, exciting and relatively easy to specify. People, on the other hand, are often seen as reactionary, resistant to change and difficult to please by computer specialists. No wonder the technical aspects of a system get top priority! But the people who are to use the system must be considered if the system is to be a success. This section looks at making sure that users are involved in systems development.

6.2.1 Reason for investigation

When an area of a business is to be investigated with a view to the implementation of a new or improved system it is good working practice for personnel to be informed of the reason for the investigation. There are many good reasons for new system development. An example of such a reason may be that the current system is outmoded and is no longer accomplishing its designated purpose or achieving its objectives. Then, in turn, the reasons for the new system must then be stated – perhaps it is important to implement it in order to become more efficient and to be able to withstand competition to enable the company to remain, or become, profitable. It is important that user department personnel are aware of the nature of the proposed system with an explanation of how it differs from the current one. Any subsequent proposals will recommend how the new system will run – its purpose, the hardware and software to be employed, timescale for implementation, etc. An example might be the implementation of an order-entry system to streamline the order handling procedure to achieve a 24 hour turnaround time which is not possible with the present order processing system. The new system may also be considered for integration with other related sub-systems to avoid entering data more than once. Using the previous example, this strategy would also have the effect of speeding up the preparation of invoices and assist in the optimisation of stock levels to minimise stock shortages whilst avoiding excessive investments in stocks.

Staff should be told that training will be provided in the new working practices. User participation creates a greater degree of awareness of the operational environment and develops more positive attitudes with enhanced job enrichment.

6.2.2 Staff participation

It is advisable to co-opt the services of personnel in the user departments who are operationally involved with the current system. This strategy is essential because of the knowledge they possess and the experience they have in operating the system. It is important that their specialised knowledge is incorporated into the new system because they also understand the idiosyncrasies, strengths and weaknesses of the current system. New systems should incorporate the strengths of the current system whilst eliminating the weaknesses. In this way a more powerful and reliable system will emerge to suit current operational needs and practices. Staff participation will also engender the necessary degree of cooperation which is essential for complex system development projects. The extent to which users participate in the design of the systems will vary with the outlook of the management of the business – its management style, whether autocratic or democratic, and the viewpoint of the trade unions regarding the interests of their membership.

6.3 STAGES OF SYSTEMS DEVELOPMENT

Here, we will look at seven stages of systems development in more detail. The actual number of stages involved is not important; some authors will mention five or eight, but the actual activities carried throughout systems development will be the same. It is simply the case that some authors combine two or more of the stages covered below, or indeed split one of the stages into more parts. The stages together form the *systems development life cycle*, so called because each system appears to have a beginning, a useful life, and then becomes obsolete and is replaced, starting the cycle over again.

Stage 1: Information strategy planning

Corporate strategy should not be considered in isolation from the supportive information systems which enable a business to function effectively. Corporate strategy needs to include long-term plans for developing and maintaining not only effective but dynamic information systems which are sufficiently integrated and flexible to keep in phase with changes in production, marketing and other business strategies. It is pointless having information systems which are not geared to producing information relating to current situations because they are inflexible and unresponsive to changing business patterns. Information strategy planning is concerned with top management's goals, critical success factors and an overview of business functions, data and information needs.

Stage 2: Business analysis

This analysis determines the processes required to operate specific areas of the business, including the degree to which these processes are interrelated, and also the data that needs to be collected and processed in order to achieve the system objectives. The data may be in machine-readable form or on paper. The ultimate effectiveness of a new system is dependent upon the depth and efficiency of analysis. This aspect is further discussed later in the chapter.

Stage 3: System design

This stage uses the information gleaned in stage 2 to define a model of the system. The model definition will include details of how the processes are to be performed, including:

> defined procedures,
> specified methods,
> the techniques to be applied, and
> the extent to which direct user involvement is required.

The data to be used will be defined in terms of its volume, format and organisation into files. All these details will be set out in a written system specification which is used in the following stages.

Stage 4: Building the system

During this stage the model is converted into a physical system in a manner analogous to that in which building plans drawn up by an architect are used by a builder to construct the building using specified materials and techniques. In respect of information systems they are constructed from the system specification and the system building may involve the use of fourth generation languages, code generators and prototyping tools.

Stage 5: System testing and implementation

The new system is installed with, probably, new equipment and procedures which may require staff to be trained in advance in readiness for live operation. Before a new information system is implemented on a wide scale a company may decide to implement a pilot scheme in one area of its business to ensure the system achieves its defined purpose and objectives. This is a fail safe procedure avoiding unnecessary disruption to other business areas. Once the pilot system has proved satisfactory it may be installed throughout all relevant areas of the business. This may apply to the implementation of on-line financial terminals in building society and bank branches.

New procedures and equipment are subjected to stringent testing to ensure they are free of technical faults prior to full installation. The results of testing are compared with precomputed results to ensure their compatibility. Differences may indicate omissions in the system design and/or logical or syntactical errors in the source code. Such errors must be rectified before the system goes on to its next stage. In addition to new system testing, parallel running of the old and new system may be advisable to avoid total disaster in the event of the new system failing to achieve its defined level of performance. The old system should be dispensed with as soon as practicable, however, to avoid unnecessary costs of running two systems side by side.

Stage 6: Systems monitoring

Newly implemented systems, although fully tested and proved to be performing satisfactorily, may nevertheless throw up a bug at a later stage when a specific routine is performed. This possibility makes it necessary to monitor the performance of the system to detect and correct any abnormalities as they arise. Problems may require amendments to the system and these can prove very costly at this stage of the system's life.

Stage 7: System maintenance

Like 'time and tide' systems are, or should be, forever dynamic to ensure they are tuned to current needs. Systems need to respond to change occurring in both the internal and external environment in which the business functions so that it is able to contend with current, rather then outmoded, situations. In any event, systems will always be subject to enhancement and amendment throughout their 'shelf-life'. They evolve quite naturally over time, and, as they evolve, they may take on different version numbers to show their different stages of major change. Changes are triggered from various sources. For example, a new version may have improved graphical facilities and may be suitable for multi-tasking, though the organisation may retain single-user versions. Change may take the form of systems integration to obtain the advantages of inputting common data once only, instead of several times as is required by separately structured functional systems. Some systems such as those dealing with financial matters, including national insurance, income tax, VAT and so on, need to be amended in accordance with current legislation, for example as indicated by the Chancellor of the Exchequer's annual budget.

6.4 STRUCTURED ANALYSIS AND DESIGN

This section describes the tools and techniques for the analysis and design stages of systems development as stated in Section 6.3. Systems development techniques were generally based on the traditional system life cycle involving the construction of flowcharts supported by complex narratives, which outlined both clerical and computer operations. The flowcharts displayed the logical sequence of processing steps but tended towards thinking in terms of physical machines and equipment rather than the logical information requirements of users.

The modern approach to the analysis and design of information systems is to adopt a structured approach – a logical *methodology* which defines in unambiguous terms WHAT a system's requirements are without considering HOW they will be physically accomplished. These logical needs are subsequently matched to physical machines, equipment and software during the physical construction of the system. A structured methodology allows users and computing professionals to participate and cooperate through all stages of development enabling the users to meet their specific requirements. It also provides for frequent walkthroughs. These are reviews which are designed to detect errors, omissions, misunderstandings and ambiguities at any stage of development. The methodology encompasses the checking of system logic during the logical analysis and design phases, in order that errors may be detected and corrected before the later stages of physical design. The logical approach allows the system developer or systems engineer to identify accurately user information needs. The structured approach replaces flowcharts and complex narratives with graphical diagrams and models, which are easier to understand. Often, these models are prepared manually. Many systems, however, are developed by the application of CASE technology. The models employ techniques such as data flow diagrams (DFDs), entity life history (ELH) diagrams and entity relationship diagrams (ERDs). These are demonstrated in Chapter 7 in relation to a simplified order processing system. For developing real-time systems, which are event-driven rather than data-driven systems, other types of diagram are required. These include state transition diagrams to model the behaviour of event-driven systems and control flow diagrams which show the interaction between discrete-valued control signals and processes. Control flows can be merged with DFDs providing an overall view of system behaviour. A structure chart is used in the design process to define software architecture, including the interfaces between program modules. A number of these diagrams, together with narratives, are included in Chapter 8.

6.4.1 Systems analysis

Systems analysis identifies the data flows, processes, problems, strengths and weaknesses of the current system. These facts are taken into account during system design and used as a basis for developing a superior system. A conceptual model is constructed from the facts obtained from the analysis and it provides an outline of the system's characteristics. These include entities, entity relationships, data flows and the processes for transforming data from one status to another. For example, a data flow indicating the quantity of an item sold to a customer related to a new data flow specifying the price of the item generated a new data flow specifying the cost of the items sold. As a further example, the process of checking stock availability can transform an order item to a back order item or a despatch item depending upon whether or not the product is in stock.

6.4.2 Systems design

As a result of systems analysis, a specification of requirements is established which is concerned with a logical view of the system, and this is then expanded into a required system specification. During systems design, technical options are then identified each providing different levels of performance, e.g. speed of response, operational flexibility, operating costs and delivery times, etc. Development staff and users discuss the various options and select the one most suitable for the circumstances. Appropriate data structures are then subjected to normalisation procedures for the purpose of separating entities and their attributes into well defined file structures. (In the context of a database this requires the separation of entities into individual tables.) Functional decomposition diagrams are used to decompose high level functions (processes) into greater levels of detail and down to what are referred to as functional primitives (detailed processes). These details are included in program specifications which are subjected to a physical design control procedure – a tuning process carried out while the design is still on paper. This ensures that the system will meet its performance objectives.

Boxes 6.1 and 6.2 give some details of two common structured methodologies which are commercially available.

6.5 REVISION NOTES

1. Engineering is the term used to describe the application of scientific principles to the analysis, design, construction and operation of machines, buildings, information systems and other structures.
2. Systems engineering is the term used to describe the whole of the system development life cycle usually applying structured analysis, design and programming methodologies.

STRUCTURED SYSTEMS ANALYSIS AND DESIGN METHOD

Structured Systems Analysis and Design Method (SSADM) is the standard methodology applied by the UK government to the systems analysis and design stages of systems engineering for developing all administrative and information systems. The method is also popular in Europe. LBMS Plc developed SSADM in conjunction with the UK government's Central Computer and Telecommunications Agency (CCTA). The CCTA accepted the LBMS methodology in January 1981.

The SSADM methodology consists of an extensive set of techniques and practices for the specification of information systems. The full version 3 of SSADM consists of three phases: feasibility, analysis and design, stages akin to those described in Section 6.3. In more detail, the stages are:

```
0 Problem definition             } Feasibility phase
1 Project definition             }

2 Analysis of the current system  }
3 Specification of requirements   } Analysis phase
4 Selection of technical options  }

5 Logical data design            }
6 Logical process design         } Design phase
7 Physical design                }
```

Note that the feasibility phase was not included in earlier releases. These stages assess the significance of the problem and the costs of improving the current system.The approach for conducting the feasibility study is the same as for conducting the analysis phase so one aids the other. The details collected during the feasibility study provide the framework for further analysis during the analysis phase.

SSADM uses three key graphical views which are discussed in Chapter 7. These are data flow diagrams, entity relationship diagrams and entity life history diagrams. As work progresses on the project the three views are cross-referenced to identify inconsistencies. SSADM requires considerable user participation in identifying problems, requirements and solutions. This is assisted by the diagrams indicated above. The method is driven by the Problems/Requirements list from which selected problems are resolved and the solutions incorporated into the 'required' system specification.

Box 6.1 Details of SSADM

3.   Systems engineering takes all viewpoints into account in order to develop the best possible system for the circumstances. This is known as the optimum system.

YOURDON STRUCTURED METHOD

In 1974 Ed Yourdon founded Yourdon Inc. to develop structured techniques for systems development and the provision of consultancy and training in the use of these techniques. The Yourdon Structured Method (YSM) was the result. It addresses the following major phases in the systems development life cycle:

Feasibility study –   Why do we need a system?
Structured analysis –   What is the problem, what policy is the system to support?
Structured design –   How to apply technology to achieve the solution.

YSM employs a number of models amongst which is what is defined as the *essential model* consisting of an *essential environmental model* and an *essential behavioural model*. The essential environmental model places the system into its real-world context. It shows the organisations, people, other systems and events to which the subject system must respond. Modelling tools used are:

Statement of Purpose – A concise high level statement that explains WHAT the system is required to do.
Context Diagram – Uses a DFD notation to show the boundary between the system and the external environment. It also focuses attention on the external systems, personnel and devices with which the system must communicate. It is interesting to note that this notation differs from that applied by LBMS Plc and SSADM. A process is shown by a circle and a datastore by two parallel lines.
Event List – Describes things that occur in the environment to which the system must respond in a predetermined manner.
Entity Relationship Diagram – Defines the various entities in a system and the relationship between them. It is a semantic modelling tool.
Text Specifications – Provide precise definitions for all data represented in the models. They bind the various models together by defining the meaning (semantics), composition (syntax) and important characteristics of data flows and stores on DFDs and context diagrams, and also entities and their relationships.

The essential behavioural model defines the responses the system must make to events in its environment. It is derived from the environment model by using a process known as 'event partitioning' and uses the following tools:

Levelled set of Data Flow Diagrams.
Process specifications – Provide a precise definition of the activity taking place inside processes shown on the lowest level.
Entity relationship diagrams.
State transition diagrams – Model the dynamic behaviour of a system, i.e. its behaviour over time.

Box 6.2 Details of YSM

4. It is good working practice for personnel affected by systems development to be informed of the reason and its objectives.
5. The services of personnel in the user departments affected by systems development should be co-opted to the development team as needed to take advantage of their knowledge and experience.
6. The stages of systems development include information strategy planning, business area analysis, system design, building the system, system implementation, system testing, system monitoring and system maintenance.
7. Structured methodology is a logical approach to establishing what a system's requirements are before deciding how they will be physically achieved.
8. Structured methodology provides frequent walkthroughs which are reviews designed to detect errors, omissions and ambiguities at any stage of development.
9. Many systems are engineered by means of CASE tools.
10. Structured methodology applies modelling techniques including data flow diagrams (DFDs), entity life history diagrams, entity relationship diagrams.
11. Systems analysis identifies data flows, processes, problems, strengths and weaknesses of the current system.
12. After systems analysis a specification of requirements is established which provides a logical view of the system.
13. SSADM is the standard methodology applied by the UK government to systems engineering projects.
14. The Yourdon Structured Method (YSM) addresses the following major phases in the systems development cycle: feasibility study, structured analysis and structured design.

6.6 SELF-TEST QUESTIONS

1. Define the term 'systems engineering'.
2. The services of personnel in the user departments affected by systems development should be co-opted to the development team. Why is this?
3. List the stages of systems development.
4. State your understanding of structured methodology.
5. What are CASE tools and what benefits do they provide?
6. What is the purpose of systems analysis?
7. Define the term 'modelling' and provide three examples of modelling techniques.
8. What is SSADM?
9. What does YSM address?

6.7 FURTHER READING

1. *Development of Business Information Systems*, Ron Anderson, Blackwell Scientific Publications: Oxford, 1989. Refer to chapters 3, 7 and 8.
2. *Data Processing, Volume 2 Information Systems and Technology*, 7th edn, M. & E. Handbooks/Pitman: London, 1990. Refer to chapters 10–14.
3. *Business Data Systems*, 4th edn, H.D. Clifton, Prentice Hall International:Hemel Hempstead, 1990. Refer to chapters 6–8.
4. *Information and Management Systems – Concepts and applications*, Mike Harry, Pitman: London, 1990. Refer to chapter 6.
5. *Structured Systems Analysis and Design Method (SSADM), Application and Context*, Ed Downs, Peter Clare, Ian Coe, Prentice Hall International: Hemel Hempstead, 1988. Refer to chapters as required.
6. *SSADM Directory of Services*, Central Computer and Telecommunications Agency (CCTA): London, 1990. Refer to required sections.

Chapter 7

System modelling techniques

INTRODUCTION AND SUMMARY

The previous chapter discussed a number of concepts for the development of information systems. This chapter addresses how system models are developed using the standard techniques of data flow diagrams (DFDs), entity relationship models (ERMs) and entity life histories (ELHs). Together these three techniques are a major part of most systems development methodologies. The chapter concludes with a discussion of first cut program design.

To elucidate the application of each technique, an example based on an order processing system is used throughout the chapter.

7.1 DATA FLOW DIAGRAMS

Data flow diagrams provide a simple graphical method of portraying a logical view of data flowing through a system. Most of the details required to develop a new system can be summarised in a data flow diagram, dispensing with the need for a long supporting narrative.

Data flow diagrams are constructed by means of symbols. Figure 7.1 portrays the symbols used in the Structured System Analysis and Design Method (SSADM), more fully discussed in Box 6.1. Other symbols may be used depending upon the proprietary methodology applied in structured systems development including those of Gane and Sarson, DeMarco and Yourdon. Whichever symbolisation is used, DFDs usually consist of four components:

entities which send or receive data flows – sources and sinks of data;
processes which transform the structure of data, but cannot create or lose data;
datastores for the short- or long-term storage of data;
data flow paths between the other components.

A key feature of DFDs is the ability to split each one into finer detail, creating a hierarchy of diagrams which can describe a system at any required level of

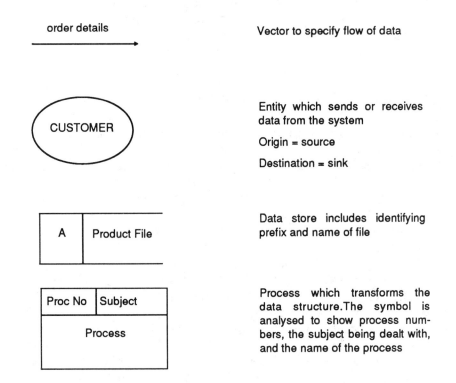

Figure 7.1 DFD symbols

detail. Different levels of diagrams can be used by different users, according to their requirements for detail about the system.

7.1.1 Interfunctional data flows

Input and output data flows and their origins and destinations are an essential requirement for data modelling and a prerequisite to the design of file structures. Data flows are recorded on a DFD together with the processes which transform data from one form to another. A DFD also highlights duplicated data and identifies data flows between related functional sub-systems. This is important because it ensures that data flows between functions are not overlooked which may be the case if an interfunctional approach is not adopted. It is essential to appreciate that data may be originated in one sub-system but used in another. For example, despatch notes may be prepared in a warehouse which supplies the data for the preparation of invoices by the invoicing system.

Further DFDs may be prepared at the design stage to indicate data flows which are required in addition to those which currently exist. A DFD also identifies entities about which information needs to be stored and pinpoints data storage aspects of the system.

7.1.2 Top-down, data-driven approach

Data flow diagrams are used in a number of ways to represent either a logical view of data flows within the current system or those relating to a proposed system. A top-down approach is often adopted for this analysis, viewing the data flows of the top level functions, e.g. those between a customer, order department, credit control, warehouse and despatch, invoicing and accounting. A DFD presents a visual representation of the elemental structure of the system and is a flexible method to adopt because it can show high level data flows and processes outlining the system in very broad terms.

These can then be analysed by the process of partitioning or levelling to provide diagrams with increasing levels of detail down to the ultimate level known as a functional primitive. The full system is then represented by a series of levelled DFDs, with the topmost level showing an overview of the entire system and the set of lowest level DFDs showing the greatest detail. Box 7.1 gives a summary of the process of constructing a DFD.

A conceptual model is a high level DFD showing entities, data flows in and out of the system, processes for transforming data, the boundary of the system and its interfaces with other related sub-systems. An entity is any subject or

a.	All processes, data flows, entities and stores should be clearly named and given identifiers.
b.	All data flows must pass through at least one process.
c.	Each process box may be broken down (decomposed) into its component, more detailed processes, determined by the functions carried out. The process is thus known as functional decomposition. Net flows in and out of the lower level DFD must equal those in and out of the process depicted at a higher level. A process numbered 1 at the first level of diagram would be broken down into processes numbered 1.1, 1.2, 1.3, etc.
d.	When constructing a DFD, it is sometimes necessary to duplicate datastores (files) and entities to avoid excessive crossover of data flow lines.
e.	Data flow diagrams should be constructed from left to right depending on the size of drawing paper used or the size of the video screen when using computerised graphical techniques.

Box 7.1 Rules for constructing a DFD

thing which requires details to be maintained during the course of business transactions. Entities include customers, suppliers, employees, order items, stock items and despatch items, etc. Where possible, conceptual models should be technology independent and people free, i.e. the details of the model should not rely either on specific ways of doing something (the technology) or on specific members of staff (the people).

7.1.3 DFDs in an order processing system

A conceptual model of a simplified order processing system is portrayed in Figure 7.2. This is constructed on the basis of the symbols shown in Figure 7.1. The conceptual model provides a thumb-nail sketch of the system which is progressively analysed into a greater depth of detail during system development.

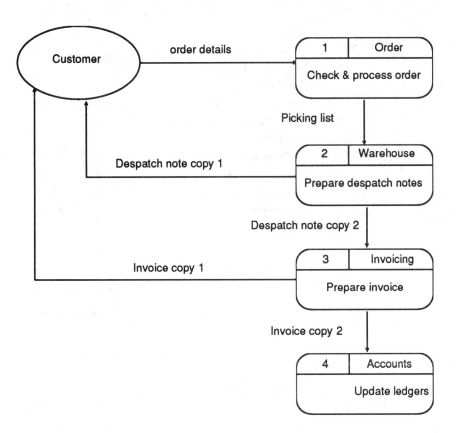

Figure 7.2 Order processing DFD

The model indicates that a customer provides details of order requirements on an order form. The order form is dealt with by the order department which passes despatch instructions to the warehouse by means of a picking list. The warehouse prepares despatch notes, one copy of which is sent to the customer and the other to the invoicing section for the preparation of an invoice. An invoice is sent to the customer to charge for the goods and a second copy is sent to the accounts department for recording the transaction on the customer's account. Not all of the entities are identified at this stage because the conceptual model only portrays an outline of the system. The system may be analysed as in Box 7.2.

Examples depicting how DFDs are typically decomposed to more detailed levels are shown in Figures 7.3 and 7.4.

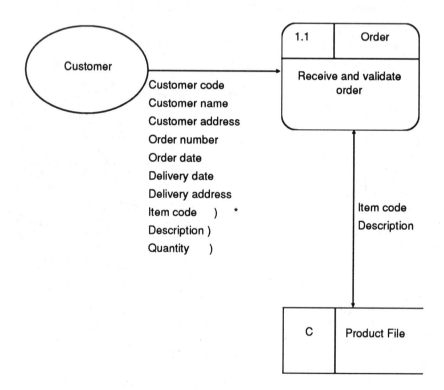

* several items may appear on the same order
(repeating group)

Figure 7.3 Order processing decomposition 1

Entity:	Customer.
Input data flows:	Order details on order form.
Transform processes:	a. Process order: check stock, prepare picking list and despatch instructions.
	b. Prepare despatch note and despatch order.
	c. Prepare invoice.
	d. Update accounts.
Output information flows:	a. Despatch instructions for items in stock (picking list).
	b. Despatch note.
	c. Invoice.
	d. Updated accounts.
Interfaces:	External customer.

Note that several processes are not shown on the conceptual model in order to maintain simplicity in demonstrating the characteristics of a conceptual model.

Box 7.2 Analysis of order processing system

7.2 ENTITY-RELATIONSHIP MODELLING

Richard Barker (see Further Reading) states that 'Information Engineering advocates looking across all information systems in a corporation to identify how information is used and shared. Program structures then are "built on top of" an enterprise-wide data model that establishes a common information infrastructure for writing the information systems used throughout a corporation. Thus, procedures follow from data and the quality of the information systems depends upon the quality of the data model.'

Information engineering makes heavy use of the concept of business or organisational entities as the basis of the data needs of a company. The relationships between those entities define the major data processing needs of the firm. Entity-relationship modelling is a technique for defining the information needs of a business. It provides a firm basis for obtaining a wide knowledge of the characteristics of a business which may be applied to the future development of information systems. An entity model (or data model) has three basic components, namely entities, relationships and attributes.

Entities

An entity is something of importance to a business about which records need to be maintained. Typical entities include materials and parts, employees, suppliers, customer accounts, invoices, functions, locations, products and assets.

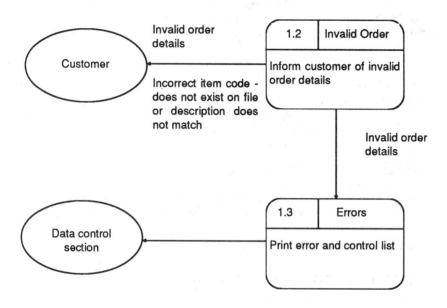

Figure 7.4 Order processing decomposition 2

Relationships

Relationships are named associations between entities. Names should indicate something of the nature of the association. Relationships also have a degree which specifies the type of relationship. There are three types of degree:

one-to-one	one occurrence of an entity is linked to one and only one occurrence of another entity;
one-to-many	one occurrence of an entity is linked to one or more occurrences of another entity;
many-to-many	many occurrences of an entity are linked to many occurrences of another entity.

Note that one in the above definitions is usually taken to include the possibility of zero, i.e. a potential relationship exists but there are no occurrences at the moment. Box 7.3 shows examples of relationships from business situations.

1. One-to-one	Each company is *run* by only one chief executive.
2. One-to-many	An employer *employs* many employees.
	One customer *receives* many invoices from a supplier.
	One customer *places* several orders.
	One order *contains* many items.
	One invoice *records* many order items.
3. Many-to-many	Many different products or services are *supplied* by many suppliers.
	Many products in a range *utilise* many of the same parts.

Italicised words suggest meaningful names for each relationship.

Box 7.3 Examples of relationships

Attributes

The descriptors of an entity are known as attributes. The attributes of an order are typically order number, date of order, order items, etc. The attributes of employee might be employee name, NI number, date joined company, etc. Attributes can be either descriptive or identifying, i.e. uniquely identifying one occurrence of an entity.

7.2.1 Entity-relationship diagrams

An entity-relationship diagram (ERD) is used for showing the relationships between different entities within the system, data entry points and access paths. Entity-relationship diagrams are used for both top-down data planning and detailed data modelling. Top-down planning identifies the principal entity types. An entity model is used to identify entry points and access paths to data. They can be developed using logical data structuring techniques (LDST), known as entity modelling, or by using the result of third normal form (3NF) data analysis. Relationships are depicted as interconnecting lines, with crow's feet or other symbolism to indicate the degree of the relationship.

The various entities which exist in an application environment will be interrelated either directly or indirectly. In order to show which entity is dependent upon another it is necessary to define which entity is a master (or owner) and which is a detail (or member). Figure 7.5 uses crow's feet pointing from the 'master entity' to the 'detail entity'. An entity which is a master in one relationship can be a detail in another as entities can exist in either role. Before entities can be precisely defined as 'master' or 'detail' it is necessary to study

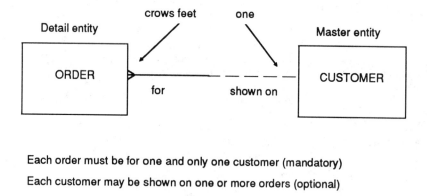

Each order must be for one and only one customer (mandatory)

Each customer may be shown on one or more orders (optional)

_____ (must be = mandatory)

— — — — (may be = optional)

Figure 7.5 Conventions for a one-to-many relationship

the operating environment in which the system functions to enable relationships to be defined precisely. It is also necessary to be aware that transaction histories show how entities change with time.

In addition a link exists between entities in the entity model and the data-stores on a data flow diagram, because, it must be remembered, entities are specific data groups which require the storage of attributes relating to them. Box 7.4 summarises the conventions for constructing an entity-relationship model.

7.2.2 Modelling the order processing system

Figure 7.6 portrays an entity-relationship core model of the order processing system. The model does not show such entities as valued orders file, picking list, despatch notes, orders file and back orders file. These are omitted in order to show primary relationships and indicate how an entity is transformed into an

1. A box represents an entity with a name in capitals.
2. An entity box may be of any size of shape of sufficient size to store the name of the entity in full and the relevant attribute details.
3. Attributes are shown in the box in lower case.
4. Two entities are associated by a relationship. See entity relationships.
5. Relationships are defined by a connected line to related entities.
6. Each relationship has two ends each of which has:
   a. a name
   b. cardinality   how many
   c. optionality   optional or mandatory

   Naming relationships at both ends helps to eliminate redundant relationships.
7. A solid line along half of the relationship is read as MUST BE which is mandatory.
8. Where the relationship end is optional a dotted line is used .
9. The crow's feet indicating the many end of a relationship line can be placed to the left or the upper end of the line.
10. An entity model may be constructed from left to right, sometimes from right to left, or from top to bottom.
11. When constructing a relational database, each entity would be a table and each attribute would become columns in the table.

Box 7.4 Conventions in constructing ERDs

entity of a different type by the occurrence of a specific event or process. This illustrates the manner of a system's behaviour when, for example, an order item becomes a stock item if it is in stock. It then becomes a despatch item and subsequently an invoice item. On the other hand, an order item remains an order item and is recorded on a back order file if it is out of stock and becomes a stock item when stocks are received. The entity relationships are analysed in Box 7.5.

7.3 ENTITY LIFE HISTORIES

Entity life histories (ELHs) are based on events (or processes) recorded in data flow diagrams and entities shown on entity-relationship diagrams. ELHs serve a number of purposes: they allow the system developer to attain an appreciation and understanding of the entities in a particular system. They are also useful for validating the details contained in DFDs assisting in the identification of missing entities or events (processes). A life history shows the chronological sequence of what occurs in a system – it does not show the structure of processes and neither is it intended to cover all the processes associated with a system, only those which update the permanent datastores (files).

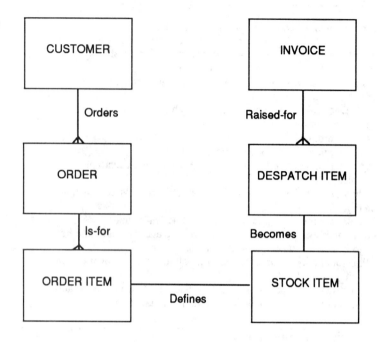

Figure 7.6 Entity relationship diagram

There are four stages in the construction of ELHs. These are:

List entities from LDS
List events from DFD
Construct an ELH matrix
Construct an ELH for each entity (see examples in Figures 7.7, 7.8).

7.3.1 Creating an entity life history

A typical life history diagram illustrating the classifications of insert (or create), modify (or amend) and delete by ELH notation is shown in Figure 7.7. Box 7.6 summarises the construction of an ELH.

Iteration

Iterations of amendments will occur for recording many items on a file and for the various types of amendment which may be specified. These iterations are indicated by an asterisk in the amendment box. The asterisk is used instead of showing a loop.

Selection

This serves the purpose of selecting an alternative course of action depending upon the condition which exists.

7.4 PROGRAM DESIGN OF ORDER PROCESSING SYSTEM

The preparation of a first cut program design in practice is a very detailed task but the details are restricted to a thumb-nail sketch in order to provide an appreciation of some of the factors involved. Any book or manual relating to SSADM provides a full account of the stages and details concerned with the task. The technique of first cut program design leads to the creation of program specifications which state what is required for processing a specific application. This is based on logical design documentation such as DFDs and ELH analysis. Physical design logic is added to the logical design factors which then become

1. Order–customer	Each order must be (mandatory) for one and only one customer.
Customer–order	Each customer may be (optional) shown on one or more orders.
2. Order item–order	Each order item must be (mandatory) for one and only one order.
Order–order item	Each order may be (optional) shown on one or more order items.
3. Stock item–order item	Each stock item must be (mandatory) for one and only one order item.
Order item–stock item	Each order item must be (mandatory) for one and only one stock item. A one–to–one relationship.
4. Despatch item–stock item	Each despatch item must be (mandatory) for one and only one stock item.
Stock item–despatch item	Each stock item must be (mandatory) for one and only one despatch item. A one–to–one relationship.
5. Despatch item–invoice	Each despatch item must be (mandatory) for one and only one invoice.
Invoice–despatch item	Each invoice may be (optional) shown on one or more despatch items.

Box 7.5 Analysis of order processing system

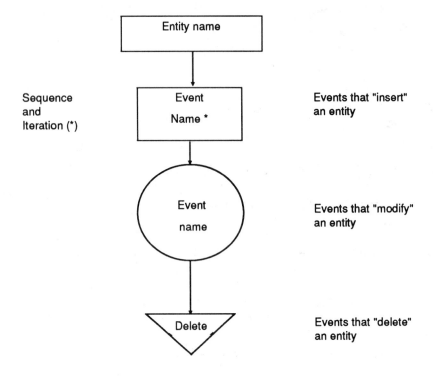

Figure 7.7 Entity life history notation

physical process specifications (PPS). Additions include details of operation requirements, human/computer interface factors including screen menus and dialogue, the logical aspects of processing data and storage requirements.

The logical design of the order processing system has physical design logic added in the form of an on-line/batch computerised system. This choice of technical options would have been decided upon at an earlier stage, based on the need to improve the efficiency of the current system to attain the required level of performance in handling orders from customers. The speedy handling of orders is an important element for improving customer relations, which is always a state to be aimed for. The current system is inefficient in this area causing backlogs which create customer dissatisfaction and cancelled orders which cause a loss of profit. Factors taken into account include details of order volumes relating to the minimum, average and maximum quantity of orders received each day and the need to attain a speedy throughput.

Although not covered in the example system, a full order processing system in practice needs to inform customers when items are out of stock to enable the

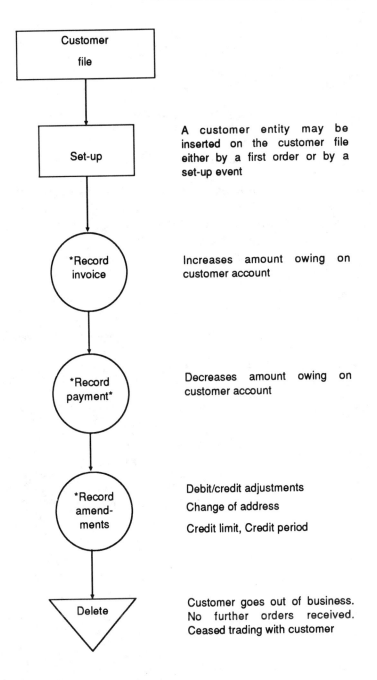

Figure 7.8 Example entity life history diagram

For each entity in a system, the following stages need to be carried out:

1. Select a specific entity from the ELH matrix.
2. Sequence the events. The ELH matrix shows the order in which events occur.
3. Define selections for alternative courses of action.
4. Define iterations for repeating a sequence of events.

Box 7.6 Stages in the construction of an ELH

substitution of suitable alternatives. This would also have the effect of improving customer relations preventing loss of revenue and profit in many instances. There is also a need to check each customer's credit before an order is accepted to prevent possible losses in respect of bad debts.

The structure of the computerised order processing system is illustrated by means of flowcharts which analyse processing tasks by means of the headings as in Box 7.7.

1.	Inputs	Data to be processed or records to be updated or referred to during processing, e.g. details of order items.
2.	Master files	Files which store records to be referred to during processing or which are to be updated. Examples are customer and product files.
3.	Processes	These are transformation operations performed on data and records such as validating, checking, computing, sorting, updating or printing
4.	Temporary files	Working files such as orders file, back orders file and valued orders file. They are used to store data temporarily during the course of processing.
5.	Outputs	The information produced by the system, e.g. error and control list, picking list, despatch note and invoice.

Box 7.7 Order processing system

7.4.1 Transaction processing

Transaction processing is to be effected by an operator using a keyboard connected to the computer. The keyboard is used to input details of order items which are validated by reference to the product file. This includes checking that the item exists on the file and that the item code agrees with the description. Errors are printed on an error report and are referred to the respective customer for correction. Corrected order items are then re-input and validated. A control listing is also produced indicating the number of orders processed and other control totals such as a hash total of order numbers. This provides a check to ensure all items have been processed. Valid items are then checked for stock availability by reference to the product file which also stores the quantity of items in stock. Items ordered and in stock update the product file by subtracting the order quantity from the quantity in stock. The items are then recorded on a temporary orders file. Items out of stock are recorded on a temporary back order file and the customer is informed of the situation.

7.4.2 Batch processing

Batch processing handles batches of order items which were stored on the orders file during on-line processing. The order file stores for each item the order number, order date, item code and quantity. The file is sorted into sequence of item code and stored on a temporary sorted file. A picking list is printed in item code sequence from the details stored on the sorted orders file. Their sequence facilitates stock picking in the warehouse where items are stored in item code sequence for ease of access. The orders file in item code sequence is re-sorted to customer code sequence so that all items for a specific order are collated for printing on despatch notes. Despatch notes are sent to customers to advise them of items which have been despatched to them. Invoice values are then computed by obtaining from the orders file the order number, item code and quantity and from the product file the item code, description, price and VAT rate. The item code is stored on both files for cross-reference and identifying specific records required for processing. Details are then recorded on a temporary valued orders file consisting of order number, item code, description, quantity, price, VAT rate, VAT, item values and invoice totals. Invoices are then printed from details stored on the valued orders file together with details from the customer file consisting of customer code, name and address. Each customer's account on the customer file is accessed to obtain the brought-forward account balance which is updated with the value of invoices. The accounts then record the current amount owing by each customer. Other procedures would be dealt with in practice such as the preparation of month-end statements of account and an analysis of sales for sales management requirements. This may include an history of sales for each customer to obtain trends and major product lines, achievements compared with targets for sales areas and sales representatives, etc.

7.5 REVISION NOTES

1. In the context of business a model is a pictorial representation of a real-world system.

2. A conceptual model is a high level data flow diagram showing entities, data flows, processes, system boundaries and interfaces with related sub-systems.

3. Data flow diagrams are constructed by means of symbols which represent entities, datastores, processes and data flow paths.

4. Data flow diagrams are used to represent a logical view of data flows within the current system or those relating to a proposed system.

5. A top-down approach is often adopted when analysing data flows commencing with top level functions. These are subsequently analysed into greater detail by the process of 'levelling' or 'partitioning' to the ultimate bottom level which is known as a 'functional primitive'.

6. The quality of an information system depends upon the quality of the data model.

7. Entity-relationship modelling is a technique for defining the information needs of a business. An entity model is used to identify entry points and access paths to data.

8. An entity diagram identifies the principal entities involved in running a business about which records need to be maintained. Typical entities are employees, customers, suppliers, functions, products, orders and stock items.

9. The details describing an 'entity' are known as 'attributes'. In the context of a relational database records are stored in 'tables' consisting of rows and columns. The columns, known as 'fields', store attributes. The rows contain a set of columns forming a 'record'.

10. Entities contained in a specific application are interrelated directly or indirectly. In order to show which entity is dependent upon another it is necessary to define which data group is a 'master' (or owner) and which is a 'detail' (or member).

11. Entity life histories are based on 'events' recorded in data flow diagrams and entity-relationship diagrams. They show in chronological sequence the events which update files. The events are insert or create, modify or amend and delete.

12. A first cut program design leads to the creation of program specifications which state what is required for processing a specific application. This is based on logical design documentation such as DFDs and ELH analysis.

13. Physical design logic is added to the logical design factors which then become physical process specifications (PPS).

7.6 SELF-TEST QUESTIONS

1. What is the purpose of a conceptual model?
2. What is a DFD and why is it useful in systems development?
3. What is the top-down approach?
4. Define the terms 'levelling' and 'functional primitive'.
5. What is the purpose of an entity diagram?
6. Define the following terms:
   (a) entity;
   (b) attributes;
   (c) tables;
   (d) fields;
   (e) record;
   (f) master;
   (g) owner.
7. What does an entity life history diagram show?

7.7 FURTHER READING

1. *Development of Business Information Systems*, Ron Anderson, Blackwell Scientific Publications: Oxford, 1989. Refer to chapters 8–10.
2. *Data Processing, Volume 2 Information Systems and Technology*, 7th edn, M. & E. Handbooks/Pitman: london, 1990. Refer to chapter 10.
3. *CASE * Method—Entity Relationship Modelling*, Richard Barker, Addison-Wesley: Wokingham, 1990. Refer to all chapters.
4. *Software Engineering*, 3rd edn, Ian Sommerville, Addison-Wesley: Wokingham, 1989. Refer to chapter 4.
5. *Business Information Systems*, Chris Clare and Peri Loucopoulos, Paradigm/Blackwell Scientific Publishing: Oxford, 1987.

Chapter 8

CASE tools and systems development

INTRODUCTION AND SUMMARY

Chapter 7 provided an overview and demonstration of analysis and design techniques for the development of systems. It is the purpose of this chapter to discuss the nature of the tools available for the automation of the various activities and modelling techniques previously discussed. Businesses today must take every opportunity to develop efficient and effective systems which accomplish a defined level of performance including quality assurance, high speed access to information and cost effective operation. In order to achieve these goals and improve the productivity of systems development an automated methodology employing CASE tools needs to be applied. This chapter also covers prototyping and fourth generation languages.

CASE is an abbreviation for either Computer-Aided Software Engineering or Computer-Aided Systems Engineering. The term 'systems' is used in some instances while the term 'software' is used in others. This is because CASE tools can be divided into two distinct categories. *Front-end CASE tools* automate activities for the preparation of system diagrams. *Back-end CASE tools* automate programming (software construction) including the generation of structured code, reporting, system testing and system maintenance. The link between back-end and front-end tools is the data dictionary, which stores system details from the analysis and design activities for later use by application generators which develop software.

Box 8.1 Definition of CASE

8.1 AUTOMATION OF THE SYSTEMS LIFE CYCLE

The system diagrams supported by most CASE tools include entity-relationship diagrams and data flow diagrams. Others support functional decomposition and entity life history diagrams, etc. The ultimate aim of CASE tools is the automation of the entire systems development life cycle through the use of screen-based graphical modelling tools. The use of CASE tools results in superior quality systems which are produced much more quickly than when using the less sophisticated and error-prone manual techniques. They check the logical consistency of diagrams relating to entity relationships and data flows and perform cross-checks between different diagramming types. These factors ensure that the user has acceptable deliverable outputs (i.e. suitable and effective software for the tasks to be performed) while management and systems developers obtain the benefits on increased productivity.

CASE tools generate increased profitability and a short pay-off period as more projects can be undertaken in a given time with the same number of staff than can be done using traditional methods. This is especially so for those CASE tools which provide multi-user facilities, allowing several developers to work concurrently on one project or several related projects.

Systems engineering often applies techniques used by the engineering industry which is based in the three stages of simplify, automate and integrate. The process of simplification often identifies common and reusable code which eliminates many repetitive tasks relating to coding and testing. Automation of the remaining simplified tasks results in higher productivity. The process of simplification or the elimination of unnecessary tasks has always been the aim of O&M analysts and this approach is used in some development tools referred to as I-CASE (Integrated-CASE) tools. They enable an unbroken path to be followed from the initial planning and analysis stages of development through the whole of the systems development life cycle. The use of I-CASE avoids the need to code programs manually AND use a single repository which integrates with front-end design tools and a back-end code generator.

Some non-integrated CASE packages generate code for parts of an application, sometimes limited to screen, report and database definitions. The remaining logic is then coded manually using a language such as Cobol. When segments of an application are coded externally from the CASE tool, two repositories of design information are created. One repository is for the storage of design specifications obtained from the planning, analysis and design tools and one is for storing code. In such cases there is no facility for automatically checking the logical consistency of the two separately implemented repositories. This must be done by the programming staff. Some non-integrated CASE tools incorporate facilities to gain access to an external code generator but this does not remove the need for two separate repositories. A repository is still needed for the design information of the CASE tool and a repository for the code generated by the external code generator.

It is important to appreciate that although CASE tools check the logical aspects of a system they do not indicate whether the systems being developed fulfil the business objectives. This is where the cooperation of user department staff is essential as they alone are in a position to provide knowledge of the needs of the system under construction thereby ensuring it meets true business requirements. User involvement provides external quality control checking which eliminates the effect of system developers omitting important elements of a system during the analysis and design stage which can create havoc, requiring systems to be reprogrammed. Quality checking by user department staff improves the quality of software on which the effective running of the system depends.

Automated development methods provide for consistency and completeness checks by searching for inconsistencies such as:

Data flows in a detailed (child) diagram not brought up to the high level diagram (parent)
Unnamed symbols
Unnumbered processes
Undesigned data flows
Dangling symbols or data flow lines (open loop)
Data flows not connected to a process
Input data flows attached to output flows
Output data flows attached to input flows.

8.1.1 Reverse engineering

A further development in the use of CASE tools is known as *reverse engineering*, the process of automatically creating abstract models that describe the action of existing computer programs. Reverse engineering tools are used to extract the essence of existing applications and store details in the dictionary of one or more CASE products. These models can then be modified and combined with similar models to form a wider model capable of supporting automated systems development and software maintenance.

Reverse engineering is employed particularly in system maintenance and enhancement and where the existing system is old and/or has not been developed and documented according to the methods described in Chapter 7. For such systems, whilst individual programs may be documented, it is often difficult to obtain an overall view of the conceptual model upon which the system is based. In the worst case, the conceptual model may not exist, but the more likely case is that the system has been altered many times during its lifetime and the original model is no longer valid.

The CASE tools which perform reverse engineering tasks actually extract information from the current systems and use this to create a new entity-relationship model. Once this has been accomplished, then the steps towards re-engineering a new or enhanced system can be taken. The tools derive the information from the existing program code, data structures, data flows and control mechanisms already stored on the computer.

8.1.2 Other methodologies and software

CASE tools are sometimes used in combination with other methodologies, techniques and software, including:

> application generators
> fourth generation languages
> data structure design techniques
> third normal form (3NF) analysis for the creation of databases
> prototyping
> action diagrams for code generation and Structured English.

The general benefits of CASE tools are development productivity increased, development costs have a shorter pay-back period, quality assurance improved and deliverable outputs in a shorter time period.

This CASE tool is from Interactive Development Environments (IDE), founded in 1983 by Anton Wasserman, and was first available in 1985. It provides an integrated, multi-user environment supporting software engineering methodologies across the entire software life cycle. The methodologies supported include:

> Structured Systems Analysis (DeMarco, Gane and Sarson);
> Real Time Requirements Specification (Hatley/Pirbhai);
> Hierarchical Data Structures (Jackson);
> Entity-Relationship Modelling (Chen);
> Structured System Design (Constantine/Yourdon).

Features of the Software Through Pictures (STP) tool are:

1. Modular architecture.
2. Multi-user, object-orientated data dictionary connecting all techniques.
3. No limits on data size, data dictionary size or number of users.
4. Configuration management and version control facilities.
5. Full concurrent usage.

Box 8.2 CASE example – Software Through Pictures

8.2 PROTOTYPING

The purpose of prototyping is to display and demonstrate the features of a system to prospective users so that they can observe what it achieves and how well, or otherwise, it provides the type of records and information required. It may subsequently be modified in accordance with user suggestions until a working system is developed which is acceptable to the user. The technique provides users with a high degree of satisfaction because applications are usually delivered and operational much sooner than conventional methods of system development. An important requirement of prototyping is the provision of a friendly interface such as a master menu and sub-menus and pop-up lists of fields and filenames enabling the system to be used in a simplified way.

8.2.1 Systems development using prototyping

Systems are usually developed by means of system development life cycle methodology applying either manual structured analysis and design techniques or CASE technology. Prototyping may be applied during any stage of the system development life cycle to allow the characteristics and features of a system to be discussed with users. This includes demonstrating what and how data is input, the processing activities which take place (although these are largely invisible) and the information, forms and reports produced. This enables amendments to be applied progressively, including the correction of errors, the elimination of anomalies and the insertion of omissions, before the system is coded.

8.2.2 Development tools

Prototyping is performed using various development tools including screen building facilities allowing the generation of default or customised screens for displaying forms in forms-based applications. This is accomplished by creating windows and painting the desired result upon the screen, choosing fields from pop-up windows and manipulating words and data through a combination of menu choices, commands and point and pick techniques. Some prototyping tools such as form and report generators produce code from details painted on the screen. Many database and file management software packages support a limited form of prototyping, particulary in the fast generation of sample menus and screens. Prototyping often utilises fourth generation languages which generate non-procedural statements, allowing the developer to describe what is wanted without having to state how it should be achieved as is the case with procedural languages such as COBOL.

8.2.3 Approaches to prototyping

Prototyping can be employed when an application is ill-defined or complex so that some initial ideas may be obtained of the nature of the application from trial and error. The nature and requirements of the system then become progressively more distinct. Prototyping may simulate the behaviour of a system for demonstration purposes, showing input procedures for entering details in a form displayed on the screen, for instance. The prototype produces predefined results from code built into the simulation program. This is purely for demonstration purposes and is incapable of processing live data.

Another prototyping methodology applies partially interactive and partially simulated elements. The interactive element accepts live data demonstrating to the user the behaviour of the system from this input. Appropriate responses, results, prompts and messages are displayed as a live system. The simulated elements may be related to end-of-day or end-of-period procedures requiring a printout of a file. As this part of the system is not coded it is simulated for demonstration purposes.

The prototype which is developed using either of the two approaches – complete simulation and partial live interactive operations combined with simulation – may be dispensed with after serving its purpose. The refined details of these prototypes may well provide the operational features and details from which to develop and code a live application – after all this is what prototyping is for. However, the prototype may also be integrated into the final system by using it as a building block rather than a blueprint. This can often save some system development time, but can also lead to difficulties later in the lifetime of the system. If the prototype is not to be reused, then the next stage is the coding of application programs by either manual means or employment of CASE tools.

8.3 FOURTH GENERATION LANGUAGES

The latest personal computers have the power to run software 250 times faster than the original IBM PC in 1981. Developments in software engineering during the same period, however, have not achieved the same increase in the speed of producing software. It is this productivity problem which heralded the creation of fourth generation languages (4GLs).

8.3.1 Nature of a 4GL

A 4GL is a high level language which allows the programmer or user to specify WHAT is to be done and not HOW it is to be done. What is to be done is written in an ultra-high-level English-like language instead of the procedural statements of a third generation language such as COBOL or BASIC. Fourth generation languages are designed to assist the use of a database regarding the insertion, retrieval, query-by-example, updating or deletion of data. A 4GL helps the developer to provide a friendly and easy to use interface between the user and the application. Creating windows, menus and screen forms facilitates the entry and retrieval of data. The extraction of information and its display in an attractive report format is also facilitated. A 4GL also speeds up the production of software. Box 8.3 summarises the requirements of a 4GL.

a.	Should enforce structure in a program which is easy to understand by other programmers.
b.	Be capable of easy modification and debugging.
c.	Must be self-documenting.
d.	Must be as close to a natural language as possible.
e.	Must be able to create windows, menus and screens.
f.	Should provide report formatting capabilities.
g.	Should provide a consistent development environment.

Box 8.3 Requirements of a 4GL

8.3.2 Database query language and SQL

Many of the first 4GLs were actually query languages added to existing database management systems. The 4GL is now an integral part of any such system. The first query language for which a standard syntax was defined was SQL from IBM, and this standard has stood the test of time and is still very much the norm for query languages. The purpose of a query language including SQL and its derivatives is to provide non-computer specialists in the various business functions, the end users, with the means to do their own information processing without having to become programming experts. The user defines the query in terms of what data is to be output, rather than the processes for getting to that output. The queries are then translated into procedural steps to produce the desired output.

An example of a simple SQL query to list all the names of the employees working in the wages section of a company might be

```
SELECT Emp-surname, Emp-inits
FROM Employee
WHERE Dept = 'Wages'
```

SQL is still a stilted syntax and takes some getting used to, but other query languages have embraced a syntax nearer to natural language. For these requirements the 4GL must be able to deal with varied syntax.

8.3.3 Query-by-example

Some databases provide the technique of 'query-by-example' so that the need to learn a formal query language to retrieve data is dispensed with. To enter a query it is necessary to type selection criteria into the appropriate columns of a screen display of a form or record selection. There is no syntax as such; the output from the query is shown by example from the selection criteria in the columns.

Multiple selection criteria can also be performed by typing the specific criteria into respective columns. For example, stock records stored in a database may consist of the attributes – part number, description, location, quantity and price. If a list is required of stock items of a specified type with a price greater than a stated amount all that would be necessary is to enter the type in the description column and the amount in the price column.

Focus, marketed by Information Builders Inc., is described as a 4GL and Database Management System with integrated tools for designing and maintaining databases.

Focus provides the following facilities:
1. Database system plus integrated tools for maintaining, designing and building databases.
2. Access and analysis of Focus and non-Focus data.
3. Full report writing, graphical output and spreadsheet software.
4. SQL support for querying data in Focus and relational format.
5. Window interface to enable end-user understanding.
6. Application development software and automatic code generation of applications so designed and developed.
7. Master dictionary of all files and fields.
8. Portability of Focus applications.

Box 8.4 CASE example – FOCUS

8.3.4 Program generators

Program generators, sometimes called application generators, are software packages which automatically generate source code such as dBASE or C which is then compiled into machine code. Generators develop systems much faster than programming applications manually. They also automatically produce system/program documentation thereby avoiding the need for this time-consuming task to be carried out by system development staff. Standardisation is also accomplished because messages are similarly structured and displayed for the various program modules thereby minimising the learning curve and the time required for program development.

Whatever programming method is used, manual or automated, it is necessary to plan the application to be developed. This requires a definition of the nature of the system, its purpose and objectives. The types of data to be input for processing must be identified together with the types of files required, the nature of the reports to be produced, the screen displays required for data entry and the types of program required to perform the logical and computational operations.

8.4 REVISION NOTES

1. Software engineering is the term used to describe the application of scientific principles and structured methodology to the efficient design, construction and operation of software for specific applications or for general use.
2. CASE is an abbreviation for Computer-Aided Systems/Software Engineering. The term 'systems' is sometimes used instead of 'software'.
3. Front-end CASE tools automate systems activities including systems analysis and design.
4. Back-end CASE tools automate programming including the generation of structured code, reporting, system testing and system maintenance.
5. The link between back-end and front-end CASE tools is the data dictionary.
6. System diagrams supported by most CASE tools include entity-relationship diagrams and data flow diagrams while others support functional decomposition and entity life history diagrams.
7. The ultimate aim of CASE tools is the automation of the whole of the systems development life cycle by the use of screen-based graphical modelling tools.
8. The use of CASE tools results in superior quality systems which are produced much more quickly than when using less sophisticated techniques.
9. Systems engineering often applies techniques used by the engineering industry which is based on the three stages of simplify, automate and integrate.
10. Although CASE tools check the logical aspects of a system they do not indicate whether the systems being developed represent what the business really needs.
11. I-CASE (Integrated-CASE) tools enable an unbroken path to be followed from the initial planning and analysis stages of development through the whole of the systems development life cycle.

12. User involvement provides external quality control checking highlighting any aspect overlooked by the system developers.
13. CASE tools are sometimes used in combination with other methodologies including application generators, fourth generation languages, data structure design techniques such as third normal form analysis, prototyping and action diagrams for code generation.
14. Reverse engineering is the process of creating abstract models that describe the action of existing computer programs.
15. The information collected from reverse engineering is useful only if it can be manipulated into new structures and relationships. This requires bridges to CASE tools, other dictionaries, databases and code generators.
16. Prototyping is a means of developing systems using various tools including screen building facilities allowing the generation of default or customised screens for displaying forms in forms-based applications. This is achieved by creating windows and painting the screen. Prototyping can be employed when an application is ill-defined to obtain some initial ideas of the nature of the application by trial and error.
17. A fourth generation language (4GL) is a high level language which allows the programmer to specify WHAT is to be done and not HOW it is to be done.
18. A 4GL states WHAT is to be done in an ultra-high-level English-like language instead of procedural statements.
19. 4GLs are used for many different purposes including prototyping languages, spreadsheets, screen painters, application generators and report generators.
20. The purpose of a query language including SQL and its derivatives is to provide non-computer specialists in the various business functions with the means to do their own processing without the need to become programmers.
21. Query-by-example (QBE) is a technique used in database applications to retrieve data by typing in selection criteria in appropriate columns of a form or record skeleton.

8.5 SELF-TEST QUESTIONS

1. What is meant by the term 'software engineering'?
2. Distinguish between 'front-end' and 'back-end' CASE tools.
3. CASE tools do not indicate whether systems being developed are what a business really wants. Discuss.
4. What is the purpose of I-CASE tools?

5. State the nature and purpose of reverse engineering.
6. Define the term 'prototyping' and indicate why it is a useful technique.
7. What is a fourth generation language and what are its main characteristics and purpose?
8. What is the purpose of a query language?
9. State what is meant by the term 'query-by-example'?
10. What is the purpose of a program generator?

8.6 FURTHER READING

1. *Software Engineering*, 3rd edn, Ian Sommerville, Addison-Wesley: Wokingham, 1989. Refer to chapters 6, 17—19.
2. *Fourth Generation Languages – Volume 1: Principles*, J. Martin, Prentice Hall: Englewood Cliffs, 1985. General reference.
3. *Fourth Generation Languages – Volume 2: Representative 4GLs*, J. Martin and J. Leben, Prentice Hall: Englewood Cliffs, 1986. General reference.
4. *Fourth Generation Languages – Volume 3: Fourth Generation Languages from IBM*, J. Martin and J. Leben, Prentice Hall: Englewood Cliffs, 1986. General reference.
5. *Application Generators Using Fourth Generation Languages*, R. Watts, NCC: Manchester, 1987. General reference.
6. *Development of Business Information Systems*, Ron Anderson, Blackwell Scientific Publications: Oxford, 1989. Refer to chapters 11—13.
7. Refer to software developers' literature for information relating to specific proprietary CASE environments.

Chapter 9

Database systems

INTRODUCTION AND SUMMARY

Database systems warrant a chapter all to themselves because they have been central to the development of many design techniques and the software to support design. The term database is also used very loosely in the computing industry, and takes on many meanings. The purpose of this chapter is to introduce and explain many of the database concepts and software packages, and note how these packages differ in their features and their user market.

9.1 DATA AND FILE MANAGEMENT PACKAGES

These are designed to enable end-users to create, store and retrieve data from computer files. In the main, these packages are designed for microcomputer users and, predominantly, single-user environments. The packages enable the user to manipulate the files with little or no need to write and code programs. They have built-in single-line commands for data access and update, and the commands are easily mastered. So, for an application with the need for few files or complex processing, the user has to engage the minimum of programming effort, yet can still produce a full software system. As the application system becomes more complex and larger in terms of the variety of data to be stored, then the need for programming help increases.

All businesses use clerical files. Information in the form of reports and summaries can be gleaned from manual files, but often this is a time-consuming task. For example, the training or personnel department will retain files of employee training. The files are usually organised by using one folder per employee. It is very simple to add a document detailing a course attended to an employee's folder. It is less simple to find out whether an individual employee has attended company policy courses B1.2, B2.2, and F1.8, since it requires searching through all the course documents. It is very awkward to find out how many employees need a refresher course in IT, and not worth the trouble to discover the number of employees who have not received any sales training in the last 18 months.

These are precisely the sorts of problems which the data management packages will address and answer in seconds. Provided that the clerical records are transferred to disk (in the form of files, records and fields), then the types of information retrieval outlined above translate into simple commands. The packages permit straightforward entry of data into files, based on screen input, and then have very powerful commands for the update, interrogation, and reporting of files. These commands are generally grouped under the term 'query language', which means that it is an interactive end-user language.

The first packages of this type which were developed revolutionised the way in which users could control and manipulate their own local data. The main player at the beginning was dBASE II from Ashton-Tate Inc. Several versions of dBASE later, the company no longer owns the product, and many other similar packages are available from other companies (e.g. Paradox, FoxPro, DataEase).

Some of these packages are (inaccurately) called database management systems or just databases. In fact, they are data or file management systems, which support some of the database concepts.

9.1.1 Features of a typical package

The principal features found in a typical database package are :

- file definition and creation;
- entering data into files;
- information retrieval from files;
- file updating;
- file prints and reports;
- a programming language for larger applications.

All the packages work on files, records and fields or data items. Each file must have identified for it a field, or group of fields, which is the key field. This is a field which, given its value, will uniquely identify one record occurrence. Where there is no such field, then one has to be added. For example, the record fields on a file of computing degrees in the country might be – course name, college/university, number of students, etc. Here, the course name will not be a key since several courses will be called 'Business Studies' or 'Computer Science'. The course name with the college name will probably provide a key, but it is a cumbersome one, full of text.

Each field must have a type, or format. This defines whether it is a field containing characters, numerics or both. This is necessary so that the package can know whether arithmetic can be performed on the field. The data types are typically:

- character or text – any keyboard character;
- numeric – numbers and decimal points only, and further sub-divided into integers and decimal numbers;
- date – containing a date in the format DDMMYY, or similar.

A sample file definition is shown in Box 9.1. The final column in the example relates to the maximum length or size of the field. It is not always necessary for the user to specify this – it depends on the package.

FILENAME: EMPLOYEE

Field Name	Type	Length
Emp-number	numeric	6
Surname	text	15
Address	text	45
Tax-code	text	5
Dept-code	numeric	4
Salary-scale	numeric	4
Sick-leave	numeric	2

Box 9.1 Sample file definition

The total size of the file is limited by the disk space available. The file definition is sometimes called the template or dictionary since it defines a shape for the record. It is an entirely separate entity from the file contents, which contain actual data in the form of record occurrences. The packages will store the file definition and the contents separately (although not necessarily in a separate file).

9.1.2 File definition

A file is defined through a series of screen prompts which ask the user to describe the characteristics of the file, its records and fields. Files need to have unique names, and field names within files must also be unique. The definition is often done in a tabular manner, as shown above.

In addition to specifying field lengths and types, some packages permit the specification of validation rules for fields. For example:

- an age field can only take values between 0 and 140;
- a department code might only take the values ACC, SALES, STORES and MGT;
- a product code is five characters long: the first two are always letters and the last three are always digits.

The software package will refuse to store any value outside the specified range and will ask the user to re-enter the value. This all helps with the validation of data input to the system and is a step towards ensuring that the data is accurate, i.e. free from known errors. However, excessive validation checks and requests for confirmation of details can slow down data input very considerably and a balance often has to be struck between avoiding errors and speed of input.

As mentioned above, the record key must be indicated. The key must be unique to a record, as any duplication may cause problems. Encoding of a field may be required to ensure uniqueness.

At the end of the file description stage, data entry may commence. The majority of packages will assume that data entry comes from the keyboard, although they will permit data to be entered from another file provided that it has a similar record format as that defined at the previous stage. There will be a command or option on a menu to select to begin data entry. The command might typically be called APPEND, or INSERT. Whether by option or command, the next thing to do is to specify the file into which the records should be added, and then the screen will display all the field names and lengths in a manner similar to that in Box 9.2.

The field values are entered into the spaces alongside the field names, in a way which is the screen equivalent of filling in paper forms. The length of each field is denoted by the [] delimiters, as a guide to entering values. When one record has all its values, the screen will display another blank record, and the user continues to add as many records as needed.

All good packages have the facility to define additional indexes on fields. As discussed in Chapter 2, an index on a disk file is functionally identical to a book or library index, i.e. it serves to provide faster access to something about which you have some knowledge. In a disk file, the index is ordered on the value of a particular field (character or numeric) and points to the record(s) on the file with that field value. The search for a record with a known field value can therefore be made more speedy by the use of an index. An index can be defined for any field on the record. Each index is held as a separate file containing field values and pointers (the number of the record in the main file) to the records with these values.

```
RECORD NO 00001

Emp-number    [    ]
Surname       [        ]
Address       [                    ]
Tax-code      [   ]
Dept-code     [   ]
Salary-scale  [   ]
Sick-leave    [ ]
```

Box 9.2 Screen display of EMPLOYEE record

9.1.3 Retrieval of data

The major advantage of these packages is not so much the ease of entering data, but rather the ease by which it can be retrieved, or interrogated. The simplest form of retrieval is to display the contents of a file on the screen. This is done through a menu option or a command such as DISPLAY or LIST. The full contents of all the records on a file can be displayed through a command such as:

LIST filename

where the name of the stored file is substituted for *filename*. Conditions can be added to the command which will better define what is wanted. For example, the following is a typical command which will extract the department code and employee number for all employees with the surname Brown or Smith.

LIST Employee dept-code, emp-number FOR surname = "Brown" or surname = "Smith"

Each package will have some additional functions for use with the LIST facility. These will be variously:

* sum values of a field;
* count number of records;
* list maximum or minimum values of a field;
* average the values of a field, and many others.

9.1.4 Updating data

The three main processes in updating are insert, amend, and delete. Insertion and deletion refer to the addition and removal of entire records from the file respectively. Amendment, on the other hand, refers to the task of altering field values within a record, and this is accomplished by replacing the current values with new ones.

Amendment of field values in records already on the file is achieved through a command such as REPLACE or EDIT or by the appropriate menu option. Amendment also encompasses the deletion of field values, which is to say making a field have a null value. This would mean putting spaces in a text field and putting zeros into a numeric one.

Deletion of a record is also very simple. However, the deletion process is frequently a two-step one. A lot of the packages work on the basis of not actually deleting the record from the file, but merely tagging it as deleted. It will not appear on a list of records on the file, but strictly it still resides on the file. It can even be undeleted. Alternatively, the second step in the process can be invoked, and the record will be removed from the file permanently. The reasons for the two-step deletion are processing convenience, to save time and to allow the user to rectify a mistake. This latter is particularly important, especially where several different people operate a single database which contains rapidly changing data. Only one person should have authority to delete data finally, after a rigorous check.

9.1.5 Print and report

This is a very similar process to retrieval, except that here the results are displayed on the printer, not on the VDU screen. The print facility is likely to be identical to that of screen display, except that the command will be PRINT instead of DISPLAY, and the layout will be identical to that on screen.

The more useful and powerful command is REPORT which permits all sorts of extra facilities to appear on paper, such as:

* headings;
* sub-headings;
* columnar format;
* totalling and sub-totalling of numeric field values;
* page numbering;
* new page for each record or group of records, etc.

9.1.6 Joining

Where an application uses two or more files, it is very difficult to perform the full update and retrieval processes purely through interactive commands of the type outlined above. However, for the purposes of reporting or retrieval from two or three files, there is generally a facility to join files together, given that they are compatible for joining. The condition for compatibility is that the files contain a common field. So the record description for each file must contain a field with the same name and format.

The act of joining two files will produce a third file which has all the fields from both files, although the software may or may not allow further manipulation of this third file. It may be stored as a *view* rather than a full file.

9.1.7 Programming language

This is a facility provided in order that full data manipulation can take place, since the query language will not be able to perform easily every possible type of process. In addition, if an application system is stable, then it is more efficient for the system to be programmed than for it to be run from interactive commands. It is a very powerful facility, and can be used to provide a more flexible screen layout for data input and update, and to perform more complex processing across several files.

9.2 DATABASE MANAGEMENT SYSTEMS (DBMSs)

The second type of database package is the full-blown multi-user set of software which has traditionally been run on the larger computers and presumes that the data in the database is used by the company or organisation as a whole, not just by one department or section.

A database approach to developing applications assumes that application systems will share data (files and records) and that application systems will be planned and developed such that their relationship with other application systems is known and utilised for the benefit of the user.

This approach arose from the recognition on the part of the computing fraternity that systems development was taking too long, that much of the data was duplicated across several applications but with different values, and that integration between systems was almost impossible. The first systems calling themselves DBMSs appeared on the market in the late 1960s and were implementations which attempted to fulfil a set of database aims. The aims are summarised in Box 9.3.

The body of data is called the database and the DBMS controls all access to the database. The DBMS has some extremely sophisticated and powerful functions which are far beyond those of other data management software. These are:

---

1.   To reduce data redundancy.
2.   To remove data inconsistency.
3.   To improve data integrity.
4.   To support data independence.
5.   To provide full recovery and security facilities for the database.

Box 9.3 Aims of a DBMS

- multi-user access to data, and control of concurrent access;
- data access control at several levels, based on a number of conditions;
- query facilities and high level languages;
- data validation by the DBMS in addition to that used in program's views of data.

It can offer all these facilities because of the structure of the database itself. It is designed in a different manner to normal files.

Multi-user access is one of the main points which distinguishes the true DBMS from smaller lookalikes. Allowing several users to access the same data (whether this be a field on a record or the entire record) has its problems. It is possible to get into the situation where two or more users want to update a record at the same time. This is called a situation of concurrency. The example in Box 9.4 serves to illustrate problems which can arise through concurrent access.

Concurrency happens only in the case where update transactions require simultaneous access. The remedy for the situation is a standard one – only permit one update transaction to be current on a record – but not all software incorporates this feature. The DBMS will cope quite easily.

The concept of views of data is simply a way of making the shared database actually appear to the user rather like it would if the system were back to the old application-dependent ways. Any one user is interested in a small part of the database for his or her job, so the DBMS has a facility for letting each user only 'see' the part of the database which he or she needs. This safeguards against retrieval or amendment of data by either intention or accident. For example, in a retail firm, the sales staff would be allowed to 'see' the order and product data. They would not be given the password to look at the salary of the directors of the firm (it is for the eyes of accounts/payroll section alone), nor would they be able to make amendments to their own pay!

Database views are illustrated in Figure 9.1. The actual structure of the database will be quite different from that of the views. The logical data structure is separate from the physical data structure.

Access to the data can be further restricted, where needed, by the provision of a facility to make data available to users according to conditions on:

Consider taking a database approach to ordering and stock control, so that the sales and warehouse sections can have an identical, up-to-date note of stock levels. Because there will be sharing of data, then the following situation could arise. Sales section accepts an order for 30 units of product P567 and decrements the quantity of stock in hand, and, virtually simultaneously, the warehouse increments the quantity on hand because it has just received a delivery of 600 units of P567. Prior to the amendments, the quantity of P567 was 64, say. The new correct value of quantity on hand should be

$$64 - 30 + 600 = 634 \text{ units.}$$

Because of the delay between reading a record, amending it in main memory and then writing it back to disk, what might happen chronologically is:

sales reads stock record for P567 (64 units)
warehouse reads stock record for P567 (64 units)
sales amends and writes stock record (64–30=34 units)
warehouse amends and writes stock record (64+600=664 units).

The quantity on hand figure is now incorrect, as the effect of the 30 unit sale has not registered. Data has been lost.

Box 9.4 Concurrency example

type of use – delete, amend, retrieve;
type of user – based on a password;
type of data – record, file, field;
time, day or date;
terminal in use.

Thus, it can be specified that the data field SALARY-GRADE can only be amended by user number SE342 sitting at terminal 56 between 16.30 and 17.00 on a Monday.

The query facilities are very useful since they support the provision of *ad hoc* requests for information from the database. In traditional file-based systems, this has to be done through a high level language program and the computing department. Hence the time delay between the request and the results.

The software for larger systems runs on a more powerful machine, with a more complex and sophisticated OS, with more complex data structures, and has correspondingly more commands than its microcomputer counterpart.

9.2.1 Security and recovery in databases

Security and recovery features are often not present in microcomputer database packages. This is often because of limitations on the size of the package and,

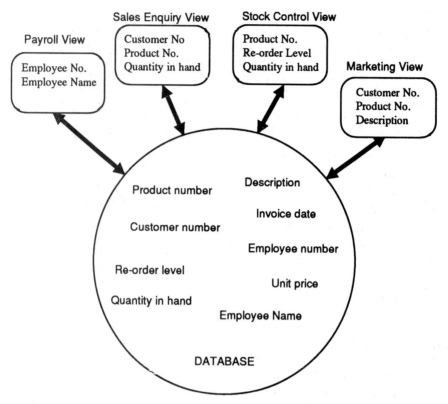

Figure 9.1 Database views

because in the environment of the micro packages, these features are not of high priority. However, in the large multi-user environment, such considerations may be crucial to the organisation.

Security

Security concerns the protection of the database from intentional or unintentional damage. Such damage can arise from:

program error (unintentional)
unauthorised amendments to programs (intentional)
unauthorised access (intentional).

In order to maintain some protection, each authorised database user has a user profile maintained on file within the DBMS. When that user attempts to access the system, the following steps are taken:

the user must identify him- or herself as a user (by login-id)
the user must verify that identification (e.g. by password).

In addition, the DBMS will check the type of access to which that user is entitled. This will already have been defined for the user by the system manager or database administrator (DBA) who manages the software (see views above). When the user attempts to access data in a manner not described by the view then the DBMS bars access.

Recovery

Recovery concerns the ability of the DBMS to restore the database to full working order after a failure has taken place. There are two types of failure, namely transaction failure and system failure.

In the case of the former, the database may not be damaged and so the system can continue to function, although the program running the transaction may halt. In the latter case, it is likely that the entire system will fail and that processing will stop on the computer.

The purpose of the DBMS recovery procedures are to restore the database to a known, consistent state prior to the failure. These procedures can be vital to an organisation. Whilst the likelihood of a full system failure is small (it is to be hoped), the length of time during which the system is not operational due to failure can be critical to the company. For example, companies which rely heavily on computers to perform their main operational activities (e.g. financial institutions, travel agencies, stock market) can lose customers and be threatened by their competitors when the computer systems are down. Such companies ensure that the systems can recover quickly.

Recovery procedures are always invoked manually, but then are effected by the DBMS. The price for having recovery mechanisms is high in terms of cost and size of the DBMS, run time, and memory, but it is up to the company using the DBMS to judge whether this is more expensive than the possible effects of computer down time.

9.3 DATABASE STRUCTURES

Large database systems require new data structures and access paths in order to carry out the processing in a correct and efficient manner. Systems modelling requires that a technology-free model of the system is defined. After the detailed and timely phase of system modelling, there follows the stage of putting the model into computing terms and actually implementing the model. There will be several ways of implementing just one system model, and, accordingly, several possible implementations. The reason for this is that implementation is dictated by the choice of hardware and software platform on which the final system will run. Depending on the machine characteristics (e.g. mainframe, micro, open system, range of peripherals) and the software to be used (e.g. programming language, database package, operating system), the actual manner in which the eventual computer system operates will vary from organisation to organisation.

One such constraint on implementation is the database approach. If database software is to be used to run the system, then the system must conform to the storage and access methods supported by the database management system. There are three very common structures used in database technology, namely hierarchies, networks and relations. Each of these structures is considered in more detail in this section and the order processing system of Chapter 7 will be used in the examples.

9.3.1 Hierarchical data structure

The entities in a hierarchy take the form of an inverted *tree* structure consisting of the main trunk from which stem main branches and which in turn have smaller branches (sub-branches) emanating from them. A customer entity, for instance, may have several order entities each of which may have several order items, as shown in Figure 9.2. Access starts at the top and proceeds downwards through the hierarchical structure. Each entity may be related to any number of entities at any level below it but only one element above it.

9.3.2 Network data structure

This type of structure is centred around the concept of a *set* which is a relationship between two record types, e.g. a customer and an order, and an order and an order item, as shown in Figure 9.3. An owner of a set, a customer for instance, can have a number of members such as orders. A record type may be a member of one set and an owner of another. An order is a member of a customer set but it is the owner of an order set having order items as members. The network defines the route through the database but the user must know what linkages exist in order to be aware of how data is to be retrieved. Links between records are through the use of pointers. An order record can point to several order item records which relate to it. Pointers inform the DBMS where the logical record is located. The next record is indicated by a *next* pointer. Within any occurrence in a set the route to be traversed is to read the *owner* and then

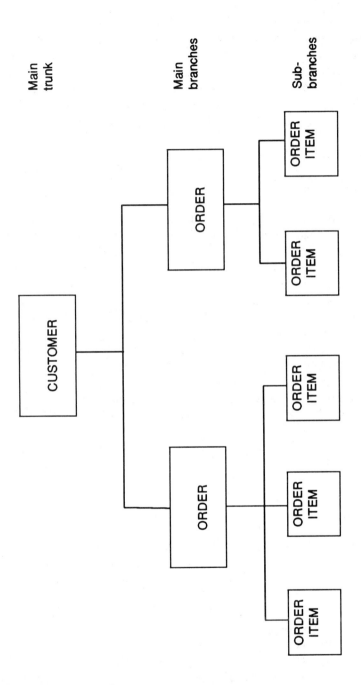

Figure 9.2 Hierarchical structure of order processing system

access the *members* sequentially, eventually returning to the owner. Most network databases utilise a complex system of pointers whereby the owner of a set can point to all of its members, each member in turn points to the next and prior member, and all members point back to the owner. Records are deleted by removing the pointers which provide the access route to a record. The links between the records on either side of the one deleted are maintained by the DBMS. The insertion of records is also accomplished by the DBMS which accesses the relevant set and enters the record in the relevant location.

9.3.3 Relational data structure

Many databases are based on relational technology whereby databases are structured on what are referred to as *relations*, two-dimensional tables of rows and columns. The columns specify the name of each attribute (or field). For example, the relation EMPLOYEE will have attributes such as surname, address, NI number, date joined company, etc.

Relational data analysis describes a relation by listing its columns. One row in the relation contains one occurrence of each attributes (comprising a record) relating to the relation and is referred to as a *tuple*. A tuple is thus one occurrence of the related column values of a relation. See Figure 9.4. The EMPLOYEE relation mentioned above could have tuples such as:

Jones, 13 Regal Avenue, YZ 12 76 83 66, 17/11/1977
MacDonald, 88A Johnson Terrace, ZF 45 65 23 12, 29/02/1984.

Thus relation, column, row are analogous to file, field, record respectively in traditional file terms.

9.3.4 Normalisation

Data models define the structure of files and assist in obtaining an appreciation of the data needs of a business. They facilitate the segregation of data into separate relations which are two-dimensional tables, as discussed above, when developing relational databases. This is accomplished by the process of *normalisation,* a technique for decomposing data structures such as entities into relations which are linked but contain no hidden data dependencies.

The entity-relationship model in Figure 7.6 would normally have an additional table specifying the attributes of each entity but this is omitted for reasons of clarity. The entities are unnormalised which means they have not been subjected to the normalisation process known as third normal form (3NF)

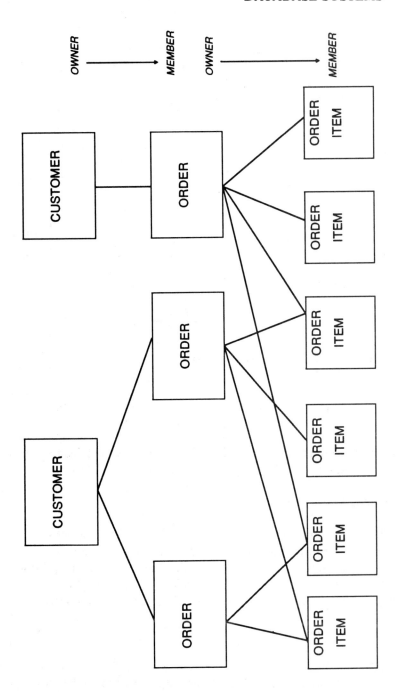

Figure 9.3 Network structure of order processing system

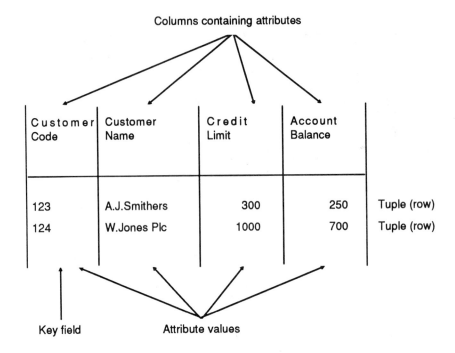

Figure 9.4 Characteristics of a relation

analysis. The principles of normalisation will now be explained and applied to the entity ORDER from the order processing system.

First normal form (1NF)

The purpose of the first normal form is to create a relation which is of fixed length and one in which all the tuples of the relation will have the same number and size of columns. In order to achieve this, any repeating groups of data must be eliminated and used to form an additional relation. Box 9.5 shows an example of the process of producing a 1NF description of an entity.

Second normal form (2NF)

This stage removes attributes which are not *functionally dependent* on the whole of a *composite* primary key. Dependency here describes a relationship between attributes where attribute A is said to be functionally dependent on attribute B

The attributes of the entity ORDER are as below. The attributes do not include the price of an item because it is deemed to be obtained from a separate PRODUCT entity.

Order number	(Key field)
Customer code	
Customer name	
Customer address	
Order date	
Delivery date	
Delivery address	
Item code }	These form a repeating
Description }	group since several items
Quantity }	may be required on each order.

First normal form requires the separation of the other attributes relating to the order as a whole, from the repeating group attributes relating to each item ordered. It is necessary, however, to include the order number for each order item for cross-reference to the order.

At this juncture we now have two records – an order record and an order item record containing attributes as follows:

ORDER

Order number	(Key field)
Customer code	
Customer name	
Customer address	
Order date	
Delivery date	
Delivery address	

ORDER ITEM

Order number	} Together form
Item code	} key field.
Description	
Quantity	

Box 9.5 Normalising ORDER to 1NF

if the value of A in a tuple is determined by the value of B. An example might be a price list consisting of a list of part numbers and prices – if the part number is known, the price is determined by the list. A composite key is one comprising two or more attributes because one attribute is not sufficient to ensure a unique key value in each tuple. Box 9.6 shows an example of 2NF normalisation.

The ORDER ITEM relation from Box 9.5 has two attributes which comprise the key, the *order number* and the *item code*. The two remaining attributes must be dependent on the key. That is, given the value of *order number* and *item code*, then the values of *description* and *quantity* are known. However, the value of the attribute *description* is predefined in any tuple by the value of the attribute *item code*. So, if the *item code* is known, the item *description* is also known. Thus *description* is not dependent on the whole of the key, and must be removed to form another relation. The resultant relations are:

ORDER
        Order number   (Key field)
        Customer code
        Customer name
        Customer address
        Order date
        Delivery date
        Delivery address

ORDER ITEM
        Order number   } Together as
        Item code   } key field.
        Quantity

STOCK ITEM
        Item code   (Key field)
        Description

Box 9.6 Normalising ORDER to 2NF

Third normal form (3NF)

The final stage removes from each relation all attributes which are dependent on other non-key attributes. Box 9.7 shows the result of the three stages of normalisation.

Note that, as a result of normalisation, all the relations have fixed length tuples, have common columns which link the relations together, and contain no implicit assumptions about relationships between the attributes. The complexity of the data appears to have increased due to the extra relations.

9.4 OBJECT-ORIENTED SYSTEMS

Many traditional software packages such as databases and expert systems are

The ORDER relation contains a *delivery address* attribute which depends upon the *customer code* (assuming the customer has a particular delivery address which is defined by the customer code and not the order number). This then results in another relation and leaves us with four entities as follows:

ORDER
       Order number   (Key field)
       Customer code
       Customer name
       Customer address
       Order date
       Delivery date
       Delivery address

ORDER ITEM
       Order number   } Together as
       Item code   } key field.
       Quantity

STOCK ITEM
       Item code   (Key field)
       Description

DEL-ADDRESS
       Customer code   (Key field)
       Delivery address

Box 9.7 Normalising ORDER to 3NF

now being developed to implement object-oriented technology. Object-oriented programming is particularly well suited to expert system development products such as expert system shells, enabling rules to be attached to objects and the use of properties such as class inheritance. The current arbitrary distinction between data, information, text and knowledge will disappear in unified single-object management systems uniting the complete range of computing platforms accessible by a universal graphics-based windows environment.

9.4.1 Objects

An object as defined by Professor Ian Sommerville (see Further Reading) is 'An entity which has a state and a defined set of operations to access and modify that state.' This means that an object consists of both data and code. The code relates to the functions or rules for processing the data. To create an object it must first have a *named class*, or a new class must be created if a suitable one does not exist. (See 9.4.2 Class.) Objects are independent and may readily be changed because all state and representation information (data and functions or data and rules) is held within the object itself. This is referred to as *encapsulation*. An object in effect is a closed system which allows changes to be made to its internal organisation as a self-contained module. Objects in fact perform operations on themselves. Access to an object by another object is not possible; therefore no deliberate or accidental use of the information it contains is possible. Changes may therefore be made without reference to other related objects. Objects may be distributed and may execute either sequentially or in parallel.

9.4.2 Object-oriented systems

Object-oriented systems address the reuse of objects, i.e. whole data structures and their associated operations, rather than building systems as combinations of isolated routines. The technique allows systems to be built from existing objects which may be called the system components. To develop object-oriented systems it is only necessary to know what an object accomplishes, not how it does it. Object-oriented systems embrace object-oriented analysis, design and programming.

Class

The basic modular unit is the *class* which represents a group of objects based on similarities. An object class is also referred to as an abstract data type (ADT), such as Motor vehicle, Account, Employee, Student, Customer, Supplier, Stock. A class describes the data structure and actions to find data. Classes are grouped together into a hierarchy commencing with general characteristics applicable to a class, e.g. motor vehicle. The general class is then analysed to specific characteristics that apply to sub-classes, e.g. cars, trucks and vans. Classes are useful to a programmer as they are a means of reusing code. A class as such is not a tangible item in itself but a template for constructing objects. The class of an object determines:

1. the name defining the nature of an object
2. the data comprising the object
3. the processes acting upon the object
4. the class from which the object is derived.

As an example object, consider a car.

Name of object:	CAR
Attributes of object:	

WITH	make	STRING
WITH	model	STRING
WITH	engine size	STRING
WITH	doors	NUMERIC
WITH	seats	NUMERIC
WITH	colour	STRING
WITH	price	NUMERIC

Processes on object:	VARIOUS

Class derived from:	MOTOR VEHICLES
Sub-class:	CARS

The term *attribute* may be defined as a data component of a class which defines its data types as shown above relating to the Class cars. The term *value* is used to indicate an instantiated attribute as indicated below relating to instances of a class. A class also provides a means of mass updating. Modifying the class definition has the effect of redefining every object that belongs to the class.

An example of a class relating to a business form is shown below:

State		
Title	:	STRING
Definer	:	PERSON
Creation-date	:	DATE
Modify-date	:	DATE
Attributes	:	ARRAY OF FIELD
Operations	:	Display
		Get-attribute-values
		Add-to-database

Using this as a template, specialised form classes can be defined as follows:

Expenses-form	:	FORM
Title	:	Expenses
Definer	:	W. Robinson
Attributes	:	Type of expense, amount of expense, expense date, total, authority
Operations	:	Complete-form, check-form, pay-expenses, store-form

Inheritance

A class may inherit the structure and methods/code from other classes without altering the nature of the originals. An example of this relates to persons and students. The class STUDENT inherits the attributes (data components) of the class PERSON.

CLASS PERSON

WITH   name   STRING
WITH   birthdate   TIME
WITH   age   NUMERIC (when needed)
        age OF person := Year(NOW) – Year(birthdate OF person)

CLASS STUDENT INHERITS person:

WITH   student id.   STRING
WITH   course   STRING

The example illustrates that the class STUDENT has similarities to the CLASS PERSON with the addition of other attributes specific to that type of class.

Instances of a class

Objects are instances of a class, i.e. specific occurrences of a class, which can be looked upon as a template for creating specific objects that behave in a similar manner. Instances of Class PERSON and Class STUDENT are:

INSTANCE person 1 ISA PERSON

WITH   name :=   William
WITH   birthdate := 10/07/1950

INSTANCE student 1 ISA STUDENT

WITH   name :=   James
WITH   birthdate :=   15/11/1962
WITH   student id.:= 124532
WITH   course IS   Information Science

Rules attaching to a class

With respect to the class STUDENT, rules for establishing the award of a specific type of grant may be stated as follows:

RULE check grant type
IF   course OF student IS Information Systems;
OR   course OF student IS Computer Science;
AND   age OF student > 21;
THEN   eligible grant IS Mature student.

Entity

Due to the commonality of attributes shared by the object types discussed above, it is indicative that a general type of object exists consisting of similar elements. This general object is called an *entity*.

9.4.3 Object-oriented design (OOD)

Object-oriented design strategy is to produce an optimum set of modules for the application being developed. These are obtained from a systematic analysis of an application area which provides the facts to establish common object types from which the modules are derived. This strategy also includes *information hiding*, a method of restricting information within design components. This allows information relating to specific objects to be changed as the need arises without affecting any other related objects. Classes are useful to the programmer as they are a way of reusing code, a way of creating many similar objects without additional effort. In order to reuse components in many systems and to enable them to be assembled efficiently the methodology must be designed for the purpose.

When developing an object-oriented design and a single instance of an object is required it should be defined directly. If a number of instantiations of an object are required an object class should be defined and the appropriate number of objects instantiated. If there is a need for the whole state to be made available outside the object, the object should be defined as an instantiation of an object class. Object-oriented design allows detailed decisions to be postponed allowing design to commence without a complete specification of requirements. Modifications can be applied as requirements are added or changed. This means that an object-oriented approach can be used to develop system prototypes which may actually evolve into the production system.

Object-oriented design is not the same as object-oriented programming.

Object-oriented languages simplify the implementation of an object-oriented design but the principle of designing a system as a set of interacting objects is distinct from implementing that system. An object-oriented design need not be implemented in an object-oriented language. The first stage in object-oriented design is to identify the entities which are part of the system and consider nouns and verbs in a natural language system description. Nouns represent objects and verbs are operations. To achieve visibility in a design, it is often useful to document it as a diagram. Diagrammatic descriptions are valuable because of their implicit impact and understanding by the observer. A network diagram may be prepared showing which objects exchange messages. This will generally be hierarchical as communication between objects is normally between a parent object and its sub-objects.

All shared data areas are eliminated as communication between objects is via message passing. This reduces overall system coupling as there is no possibility of unexpected modifications to shared information. Object-oriented systems reduce the time required to develop an application thereby increasing productivity and lower costs. Other benefits include extendability, portability and reliability.

9.4.4 Object-oriented programming (OOP)

OOP makes it possible to represent a system by defining it in terms of a structure of objects with attributes. Rules, procedures, programming calls and triggering actions can also be attached to objects. As well as being a powerful and concise way of presenting the elements of a system, OOP not only makes possible the complete separation of object definition from code but may lead to a major reduction or elimination of code replacing it with structures of objects passing messages to one another to initiate action on objects.

The approach to programming in object-oriented systems is different to the traditional approach adopted by procedural languages. Object-oriented systems are conversant with the functional requirements of processing or acting on data; they only need to know what is required, not how to do it. Traditional programming on the other hand must include in the program what to do (the operations and procedures), what to do it to (the operand), and how to do it (the technique).

The fundamental requirement is for the programmer to build effective software models of real-world situations so that events can be dealt with in a highly productive manner. A language is object based if it has the bundles of data and code which are known as objects. It is class based if it has classes which are collections of similar objects. Software construction is viewed as the assembly of existing classes. Languages exist which allow the programmer to create new objects by copying an existing object.

Polymorphism and messages

Polymorphism is a biological term meaning the occurrence of different forms, stages or colour types in organisms of the same species. In the context of this subject it relates to the same message behaving in many different ways according to the object receiving it. To cause a problem a message would have to be passed to an object for which it was not intended.

9.5 REVISION NOTES

1.   Microcomputer database packages enable end-users to create, store and retrieve data from computer files.
2.   These packages require little or no programming skills from the user.
3.   The major features include file definition and creation, data entry, information retrieval, file updating and reporting, programming language.
4.   All the features can be operated from a set of screen prompts.
5.   Large database management systems are for multi-user use and incorporate the concept of shared data.
6.   Database systems aim to reduce redundancy and inconsistency in data, and to support data independence, recovery and security of the system.
7.   A database view is a virtual file, a sub-set of the data stored on the database.
8.   Concurrency control is needed in the multi-user environment to ensure that updates are not lost.
9.   An 'object' can be described as an 'entity' which may be a person, a vehicle, customer, stock item or anything consisting of both data and code. The code relates to the functions or rules for processing the data. When object types have a commonality of attributes it is indicative that a general type of object exists which is called an entity.
10. To create an object it must first have a named class which is a group of objects based on similarities. Classes are useful to a programmer as they allow the reuse of code. A class is not a tangible item in itself but a template for constructing objects. An object is an *instance*, i.e. a specific occurrence of a class which has specific values (data). Data and actions (functions) can be shared with other objects by means of instances and *inheritance*. This means that a class may inherit the structure and code from other classes.
11. Modifying a class definition has the effect of redefining every object that belongs to the class.
12. Information hiding is a method of restricting access to information within

design components. This allows information relating to specific objects to be changed as the need arises without affecting any other related objects.

13. Object-oriented languages simplify the implementation of an object-oriented design but the principle of designing a system as a set of interacting objects is distinct from implementing the system.

14. When designing an object-oriented system the first stage is to identify the entities. The system is described by nouns to represent objects and verbs to define operations.

15. Object-oriented programming allows the complete separation of object definition from code and often leads to a reduction or elimination of code replacing it with structures of objects passing messages to each other to initiate action on objects.

16. Object-oriented systems only need to know what is required, not how to do it, as they are conversant with the function requirements which are built into the objects. Traditional programming, on the other hand, must include in the program what to do (operations and procedures), what to do it to (the operand or data) and how to do it (the processing method or technique).

17. An object-oriented language is object based if it has the bundles of data and code which are known as objects. It is class based if it has classes which are collections of similar objects.

18. In the context of object-oriented systems the term polymorphism relates to the same message behaving in many different ways according to the object receiving it.

9.6 SELF-TEST QUESTIONS

1. What is a database?
2. What is a database management system?
3. What do recovery features support?
4. What are the differences between the small and large database packages?
5. What is an 'object'?
6. State the meaning of the term 'class'.
7. State the meaning of the term 'instance'.
8. What is meant by 'information hiding'?
9. What is the first requirement when designing an object-oriented system?
10. Object-oriented systems only need to know what is required, not how to do it. Why is this?

9.7 FURTHER READING

1. *Software Engineering*, 3rd edn, Ian Sommerville, Addison-Wesley: Wokingham, 1989. Refer to chapter 11.
2. *Object Oriented Program Design*,   Mark Mullen, Addison-Wesley: Wokingham, 1989. Refer to all chapters. Gives examples in C++.
3. *An End-Users Guide to Database*, James Martin, Prentice-Hall: Englewood Cliffs, 1984.

Chapter 10

Knowledge-based systems

INTRODUCTION AND SUMMARY

The previous chapters considered the various aspects of data, information, information systems and systems engineering. This chapter discusses the primary concepts of knowledge-based systems (KBSs), a branch of artificial intelligence (AI), before discussing the nature and characteristics of expert systems in particular. Knowledge-based systems allow computers to accept knowledge from an external source and to store, access and use that knowledge through software-simulated thought and reasoning processes to solve problems or to make recommendations on probable solutions.

10.1 KNOWLEDGE-BASED SYSTEMS

An important element of any AI application is knowledge. Knowledge consists of facts relating to what has been discovered, inferred, learned, perceived and understood in respect of a specific subject. Knowledge can be obtained free from many sources, including specialist journals, public on-line databases and information systems, and published statistics. It takes many forms and includes quantitative facts used in computations, facts generated by business operations, decision-support systems, executive information systems, spreadsheets, and simulation work involving queueing theory or critical path analysis.

A knowledge-based system stores, manipulates and retrieves data in the form of knowledge about specific areas of interest called *domains*. Domains can be of any type and some examples of KBS are given later. Whilst the use of KBS is still in its infancy in organisations, they will play an increasingly important role in the business applications of computers.

10.1.1 Traditional computing vs KBS

Data input to traditional computerised information systems is processed in a defined sequence by procedural programming languages, such as COBOL or PL/1, which are composed into programs consisting of sequences of predefined instructions or statements. Knowledge-based systems define the sequence in which rules should be executed, based on available facts in the computer system. They are designed to make judgements and arrive at conclusions rather than process data by a set procedural routine. Most businesses have processes which are based on rules and company policies which can be processed by a knowledge-based system. Some KBSs, such as expert systems, can be embedded into existing procedural application programs or invoked from procedural programs. This enhances and increases the power of procedural applications by adding judgement capabilities to the normal processing routines.

10.2 KBS ARCHITECTURE

The essential features are

> the knowledge base;
> the inference engine;
> the database.

Just as a database contains a representation of real data, either by holding actual text and values or by encoding the data, the knowledge base contains a representation of the knowledge. Knowledge representation is a more complex activity since knowledge may not be termed in an absolute manner.

10.2.1 Knowledge base

A knowledge base is the heart of a KBS and it stores rules and relationships in respect of a particular problem or subject area. A production rule always has the format:

> IF x   THEN y.

The IF part is a premise and the THEN part refers to the conclusions or consequences. The premise may be a single condition or it may be compounded, and the conclusions may also be compounded.

The knowledge base may contain many such rules. Each rule may in itself be quite simple, but the power of the system lies in its ability to apply rules in groups without having a preordained order of application, as is the case in information systems.

The conclusion side of the rule may also contain a certainty factor which enables the inference engine to define probabilities in diagnostic systems.

10.2.2 Inference engine

This part of the system performs the reasoning function by interpreting rules. Initially it checks the database to determine whether an hypothesis exists. If the hypothesis is present it is accepted as a proven fact requiring no further processing. Often, however, the hypothesis does not exist and the problem must be resolved by inferencing. In this case the inference engine examines the rules in the knowledge base in a particular sequence searching for matches to the details stored in the current database. As such rules are found, they are fired, thereby implementing the specified course of action. As matching proceeds, the rules continue to fire and reference each other to form an inference chain. On each occasion that a new rule is examined, it is checked against the current status of the application or problem stored in the database. The firing of a particular rule may add new facts to the database. The process continues until a conclusion is reached. The inference engine may be able to communicate with the existing corporate database, programs or files in the process of seeking its goal.

In a KBS there has to be a notation or method of representing the knowledge for the particular domain of expertise chosen. The most common is the production rule notation, though semantic nets and frames are the other two most important notations.

10.2.3 Database

The database is the working memory of a KBS. It sometimes stores the hypothesis. It stores the initial states or conditions of the problem to be solved, including a starting point to begin the search process. It also stores facts input by the user during a consultation.

10.3 KNOWLEDGE ENGINEERING

KBS are developed by knowledge engineering (cf. systems engineering) which employs techniques embracing activities concerned with collecting, assimilating, structuring, storing and retrieving knowledge. Knowledge is collected from experts in a particular field who are known as domain experts. They disseminate their knowledge to analysts who are known as knowledge engineers.

Effectively, the traditional systems life cycle model is the one used in the development of expert systems. Perhaps this is more evident in a KBS, since clearly all knowledge and rules must be fully investigated, analysed and specified prior to implementation. However, the difficulties normally encountered by any user in understanding the system specification and requirements are multiplied many-fold with a KBS. Neither the user nor the expert informant may be in a position to question the findings of the knowledge engineer. Thus, the practice of prototyping is prevalent in knowledge engineering. Most KBS that have been introduced into an industrial setting have been developed using the prototyping approach, enabling users to see and comment on the end product as it evolves.

The feasibility study at the front-end of the systems life cycle is also very important in the development of a KBS. There are millions and millions of systems capable of computerisation, and only a small percentage of those really require a KBS. Thus, the first question to ask in a proposed KBS project is – is a KBS really necessary? To require the KBS approach, the problem domain must

- contain uncertainty;
- be one where an expert is available.

Even then it may still not require the KBS approach.

All facts and rules are built into a KBS using software such as an expert system shell or by means of specialist languages such as LISP and Prolog.

10.3.1 Knowledge elicitation

This is a huge field of study, and indeed has its own small band of experts in the problem domain. Once it has been established that a KBS is required, then the expertise in the problem domain must be entered into the new system. In a KBS, it is most likely that the knowledge will come from a human expert rather than from any written or computer data. Thus the task of the knowledge engineer in eliciting this knowledge is a formidable one and involves many hours of dialogue with the expert. The expert is most unlikely to have any experience of development of computer systems and, in particular, of the development of a KBS.

Information systems depend on the application of algorithms (in programs) to data for the processing of the data and output of information. Most experts are unable to describe algorithms which they apply to all cases in their domain of expertise. Thus, new techniques for eliciting that expertise are required.

Firstly, the dialogue between engineer and expert must concentrate on eliciting how the expert comes to particular conclusions and what knowledge is used in so doing. However, large questions of the 'How do you diagnose hepatitis?' variety are useless. The knowledge must be elicited in smaller units. It is then written down, probably in a production rule format, using English and then Structured English as the rules become more complex.

Entity-relationship analysis and normalisation techniques can also be used in the design and implementation of the KBS.

Collecting knowledge from experts is a slow process because, in many instances, human experts are not very efficient in explaining the way in which they arrive at conclusions and make decisions. Because of this, a process of data analysis is used in many instances. This method of collecting knowledge applies to a large group of expert systems such as those of a financial nature where data already exists in the organisation, e.g. within databases, archives and other computer files. It is then a matter of selecting the appropriate data for formulating rules.

10.3.2 Knowledge representation

A number of knowledge representation schemes exist which have common characteristics. They are designed so that the knowledge can be used in the reasoning process. The knowledge base stores data structures which can be processed by an inference system using search and pattern matching techniques. Knowledge representation can be either declarative or procedural. Declarative knowledge representation includes logic, semantic networks, frames and scripts, while procedural logic includes procedures and production rules. Readers wishing to study the topics of semantic networks, frames and scripts in greater detail are recommended to refer to books relating to artificial intelligence. A number of titles are provided at the end of the chapter for this purpose.

10.3.3 Logic

Logic is concerned with the process of reasoning based on a study of *propositions* (a statement that is either true or false) and their analysis in making deductions (arriving at a conclusion by the process of reasoning). Reasoning is the process of drawing conclusions from facts, observations or hypotheses. Inferencing is the process of reaching a decision by reasoning or arriving at conclusions from premises (conditions) or facts (evidence).

Box 10.1 represents a summary of terms and is fundamental to an understanding of KBS development.

Reasoning has already been defined as the process of drawing conclusions

Term	Meaning
Logic	The process of reasoning based on a study of propositions.
Proposition	A statement that is either true (T) or false (F).
Deduction	Arriving at a conclusion by the process of reasoning.
Reasoning	The process of drawing conclusions from facts, observations or hypotheses.
Inferencing	The process of reaching a decision by reasoning or arriving at a conclusion from premises or facts.
Premise	A condition which exists within the problem under consideration.
Facts	Data or evidence relating to a specific problem.
Hypothesis	A statement that is subject to being proved. An assumption on the basis of which action is taken.

A typical example of a premise and a conclusion might be:

IF	the quantity in stock of item x is equal to or less than the reorder level;
THEN	place an order to replenish stock.

IF	the quantity ordered by a customer is greater than 100;
THEN	Give a discount of 5%.

This is the way in which *production rules* are constructed.

Box 10.1 Summary of logic terms

from facts, observations or hypotheses. Two types of reasoning are used in logic, namely deductive and inductive.

Deductive reasoning

The deductive process begins with a syllogism which is a method of deductive reasoning made up of a major premise, a minor premise and a conclusion. Almost any problem can be structured in this way.

Backward chaining is a problem-solving strategy applying deductive reasoning. The method is goal driven, commencing from the goal (conclusion) and working backwards along the chain of a logical argument (conditions and statements) in an attempt to prove the conclusion by looking for facts and rules that support the required outcome. The conclusion must be valid if the premises are true. The aim is to develop new knowledge relating to a problem from previously known facts.

Goal-directed reasoning is frequently used for classification-type problems, for example the selection of personnel by matching the attributes of applicants with those ideally specified for a particular post or job. Box 10.2 gives an example pertaining to a stock control system.

Major premise

> Stocks are not reordered unless the quantity in stock (of a specific item) is equal to, or less than, the reorder quantity.

Minor premise

> The stock is in excess of the reorder quantity.

Conclusion

> The stock will not be reordered.

Box 10.2 Example of deductive reasoning

Inductive reasoning

Inductive reasoning uses established facts or premises to arrive at a conclusion. A syllogism is also used to state the nature of the problem.

Forward chaining is a problem-solving strategy used in production-rule-based systems applying inductive reasoning where conclusions are established by starting with known facts. It is a search procedure or reasoning process where known facts are used to produce new facts and reach a final conclusion. It commences with the first rule in the knowledge base. If the antecedent of the rule (the IF part) is TRUE, then the consequent (the THEN part) of the rule is used to search for a rule with a matching antecedent. The process continues until the inference mechanism fails or until it succeeds in proving a final conclusion. For example, this method could be applied by a financial institution in assessing the suitability of granting a loan to an applicant.

Unless all possible facts are included in the premises an element of uncertainty will exist in the validity of the conclusion. The level of uncertainty will be inversely proportional to the number of facts taken into account. This means that the greater the number of facts taken into consideration, the lower the level of uncertainty. The fewer the number of facts taken into account, the higher the level of uncertainty. This must be considered in the context of the number of facts taken into account in relation to the number of facts which should be taken into consideration in arriving at an acceptable conclusion. New facts may also modify conclusions previously arrived at.

In the previous example, it is stated in premise 1 that excessive overheads reduce profits. In most instances this is true, but in others it is false. It is not a

Here the problem relates to the use of business resources in respect of the efficient control of overheads, the utilisation of materials and labour productivity:

Premise 1   Excessive overheads reduce profit.

Premise 2   Excessive material usage increases costs.

Premise 3   Low labour productivity increases costs.

Conclusion   Inefficient utilisation of resources increases costs and reduces profits.

Box 10.3 Example of inductive reasoning

fact unless the overheads are analysed into fixed and variable. Fixed overheads are those relating to rent, rates, insurance premiums, heating and lighting, maintenance costs and depreciation of machines, plant and equipment which remain constant irrespective of the level of activity or volume of production. This does not complete the picture, however, because fixed overheads can increase if additional production capacity is required necessitating an extension to the factory. In respect of an insurance company, for instance, more office space may be required due to an increase in the level of business. In both cases the level of overheads must be related to the changes in business operations. The fixed overhead per unit of production is inversely proportional to the number of units produced. Variable overheads are those which are incurred in the manufacturing process and include consumable materials – oil and grease, cotton waste, cutting tools and electrical power for running machines, etc. This class of overhead varies in total in direct proportion to the level of activity but is constant per unit produced. Thus the example can be re-stated (Box 10.4).

Premise 1a.   Excessive fixed overheads decrease profit unless incurred to increase factory or office facilities because of an increase in the level of business (activity).

(Note: The overheads are not excessive in this case but are additional due to the higher level of business activity.)

Premise 1b.   Excessive fixed overheads decrease profit for normal levels of activity.

Box 10.4 Example of inductive reasoning (cont.)

Goal

At this point it is relevant to state what is meant by the term goal. In general, goals may be stated to be targets to be achieved in pursuit of specific aims. An organisation normally has a number of goals relating to various aspects of business, such as a specified level of performance in the use of resources and sales targets to be achieved. Unless all the goals are accomplished the overall business objective will fail to be achieved. In logical terms, a goal is a conclusion that the knowledge-based system (an expert system in particular) is designed to achieve during a consultation. Examples include:

> Approve mortgage request
> Deny mortgage request
> Approve capital investment
> Disapprove capital investment

10.4 EXPERT SYSTEMS

There is no single definition of an expert system, but it is the most typical example of a knowledge-basedd system. These systems are easier to describe than to define. An expert system should have the decision-making powers of a human expert in a particular field of expertise. It thus must have access to the same depth and breadth of knowledge (the knowledge base) and be capable of carrying out the reasoning in the same manner (the inference engine). Indeed, the more sophisticated expert systems actually 'learn' more about the field of expertise or the reasoning as the system is used, just as an expert can increase his or her expertise through case history and experience.

It is important to appreciate that the term *expert* does not necessarily imply a highly intellectual domain or subject area, nor does it reflect the importance of a decision, problem or task. The term should be interpreted to mean the specialised knowledge a skilled person has of a specific subject, whatever the area of expertise. Thus an expert system can be just as appropriate based on a highly skilled operator of a complex industrial plant as for a medical application.

10.4.1 Expert system applications

Early knowledge-based systems were developed mainly at major universities such as Stanford and the Massachusetts Institute of Technology (MIT). Systems were developed for diverse areas of knowledge including medical diagnosis

(MYCIN), geology in respect of the evaluation of mineral deposits (PROSPECTOR), and others in domains such as military science, process control, chemistry, information management, computer systems and electronics.

MYCIN

MYCIN was developed by Edward Shortliffe of Stanford University in the mid-1970s. The system is a medical advisor system for diagnosing bacterial infections and recommending appropriate treatment.

PROSPECTOR

PROSPECTOR is an expert system which assists geologists to locate ore deposits. Its knowledge base contains rules and heuristic data obtained from empirical data and the taxonomy of different types of minerals. Knowledge relating to different types of ore deposits was obtained from interviewing many geologists. Geologists searching for ore deposits provide the expert system with information of the terrain being explored. The expert system then evaluates the data and provides a recommendation indicating the prospects of continuing exploration of the designated area.

Business applications

The type of business and the nature of the applications which can benefit from the use of an expert system are many and varied. It is of significance that any application unsuitable for processing by procedural languages is a likely candidate for processing by a knowledge-based system. It is the aim of many organisations to implement expert systems in all suitable application areas. Personnel in the various functions are then able to obtain the knowledge of experts built into a specific application area. Expert systems cover a wide spectrum of subjects ranging from a payroll procedure for computing wages, to the rules for granting loans to employees or clients, or the pricing policy to be adopted as a marketing strategy.

Technical applications

It is important to appreciate that expert systems are used for a wide range of applications of a technical nature as distinct from those of a business and administrative nature. Some manufacturing processes collect data from sensors which specify the state of the system at any point in time. Such systems are controlled by adjusting various mechanisms to modify the controlled variable whether temperature, rate of flow, depth of cut, speed, etc. When expert systems are implemented to control such processes it is possible that the nature of the control systems and sensors will need to be reconsidered. This may necessitate the installation of new sensors for capturing data in the form and frequency required for effective control of the process.

10.4.2 Expert system shells and generators

An expert system shell is a special type of software for building expert systems that provides a framework in which data and knowledge can be entered to a knowledge base. It is important to appreciate that the shell does not contain a knowledge base of its own, since these are developed specifically for each expert system. Many shells are rule based applying the IF–THEN rule structure. Some shells allow rules to be typed in as notes or full sentences and do not require syntax, a rule language, or compilation. A dictionary can be used to copy and select rules, and full text and graphic screens provide facilities for displaying answers, advice or questions. Logical operators can be used in any combination at any level of the structure. Some shells have a menu interface, and some have facilities for linking with other mathematical calculations or to a natural language processor. The evidence behind any conclusion is explained, as is the reasoning behind any question which allows the user to explore or navigate through the entire logic of the system.

An expert system generator is similar to a shell, but it has an editor, allowing knowledge to be input in a predetermined rule format and amended as necessary. Some generators act as a compiler for compiling rules into the code the inference engine will require when processing them.

10.4.3 Expert system languages

Instead of developing expert systems by an expert system shell it is possible to program them directly using an appropriate language. Expert systems have been developed using a variety of different languages, but LISP has generally been used in America and PROLOG in Europe.

LISP

LISP is an acronym for LISt Processing and was developed in the late 1950s by John McCarthy at MIT. It is considered to be one of the most important languages for artificial intelligence applications. It is a symbolic processing language that represents information in lists. Objects such as machines, customers, suppliers and employees are represented by names or symbols. Related objects are combined to form a data structure called a list. The language has procedures to perform a wide range of operations on lists including arithmetic computations. The basic data elements in LISP are *atoms* of two types – numbers and symbols. Numbers in turn can be integer (whole number) and real (floating point or decimal) and may be positive or negative. Symbols are words that represent objects, as stated above, consisting of letters and numbers. LISP does not process individual atoms; therefore several atoms must be joined to form a *list*, a sequence of multiple atoms grouped together. The list contains atoms that usually have something in common. The following are examples of lists:

> COLOURS (blue, red, gold, silver)
> CUSTOMER CODE (X123, X124, X125)
> NAMES (Smith, Jones).

PROLOG

Prolog is a declarative language but most implementations include procedural features for dealing with arithmetic and input/output operations, etc. Three basic steps are necessary when writing programs, which relate to the characteristics and methodology of expert systems. The first two stages describe the creation of a Prolog database and the third indicates how Prolog sets about answering questions. The stages are:

1. Define objects and state their relationships.
2. Create rules that define relationships about objects.
3. Ask questions relating to objects and their relationships.

Programming in Prolog is not in the form of procedural statements but in the form of facts and rules about a specific subject which will be used to provide an answer or reach a conclusion. The facts are called clauses (or statements) which name one or more objects and state a relationship. A statement of a simple fact can be defined as follows:

> rents(bill, flat).

The first word in the fact is the predicate, which defines the relationship between the two arguments shown in parentheses. All the words in the expression are typed in lower case letters including proper names like Bill (William). When converted into English the simple fact can be interpreted to mean 'Bill rents his flat'. When a database has been established it can be used to obtain answers to questions such as 'Does Bill rent his flat?' The question would be entered as follows:

rents(bill, flat)?

Instead of a period at the end of the clause a question mark is used to indicate that a question is being asked. In some implementations the question mark appears at the beginning of the clause.

It is not possible to delve further into the fascinating subject of languages but many works of reference are available for further study for readers wishing to pursue the subject.

10.4.4 Expert systems and information systems

It is difficult to distinguish between these types of system, although it is relatively easy to distinguish one from the other when studying sample systems. An expert system is less well defined than an information system. It handles incomplete or imprecise information, it must respond to changing environments, it is concerned with making judgements and it will have no obvious path or trail that can be followed from inputs to conclusions.

An expert system is not one which uses a mathematical or statistical representation of a problem as, for example, may happen in some systems where statistical databases are used in medical diagnosis.

Some information systems employ sophisticated dialogues with users to prompt them for information and data, but they are not expert systems because they are simply carrying out processing rules in a predefined (programmed) order. Help systems can appear to be expert because the best ones are 'context sensitive' and provide help pertaining to the current decisions available to the user on a screen. However, these are not applying reasoning to the situation; the help information is linked to particular screens in a programmed manner.

10.5 MACHINE LEARNING

One of the major problems with KBS is knowledge acquisition – getting knowledge into the machine. Knowledge engineering (as discussed in Section 10.3 above) requires a human expert who provides the rules upon which deductions are based. The process is time consuming and prone to error (humans being humans) and thus costly. It may even be impossible to get a human expert to explain why he or she makes a judgement; experts often cannot elucidate their reasoning process. But they are more likely to be 'right' than others – that is what makes them expert.

One way round this problem would be to get the machine to assimilate information on its own. If a machine could *learn* like a human, the knowledge acquisition process would be much simpler. Start with an empty machine, get it to learn about some topic or other, then use its knowledge to solve problems.

Unfortunately, things are not that easy. Think back to when you were a toddler or consider how parents treat a child you know. A young child fits the description of 'an empty machine' in some ways. Once the child has mastered the rudiments of making noises, it is taught to speak by a combination of rote learning – repetition of sounds made by parents – and induction from lots of examples (see Box 10.5).

Parents do not explain to a child that 'This is an omnivorous quadrupedal mammal of the genus *Canis* and variety mongrel'; they point and say 'dog' many times.

The child somehow learns the features of a dog without being able to count to four or understand about mammalian features such as suckling young. It will then observe and experiment by trying itself to say 'dog' for other objects, at which point parents will reinforce the learning by praise or correction.

Box 10.5 Early learning

This short description highlights some of the problems which face those attempting to build machines which can learn. At least six types of learning process can be identified (O'Shea *et al.*, 1987):

rote learning
explanation
analogy
induction from examples
observation
experiment and discovery

Which of these is most appropriate to a specific machine is not known – and perhaps is unknowable. The rote learning and explanation routes are equivalent to knowledge engineering, i.e. what we are trying to avoid, so the machine will have to try the other methods. But it turns out that these processes are imperfectly understood for humans, let alone being able to write a program for a dumb machine. How does a child of 2 or 3 years recognise a Great Dane as a dog after being taught on common varieties such as mongrels and terriers? The child cannot explain and by the time it is old enough to explain, it will have learned rules and 'forgotten' how it used to identify dogs.

10.5.1 A model of the learning process

O'Shea et al. (1987) describe a simple model of the learning process which

A friend's son could, at the age of 2, identify Hillman Avenger cars at 'fifty paces'. Of course that is not what he said. Cars were either 'Tom's vroom-vroom' (a neighbour's Avenger), 'like Tom's vroom-vroom' (same model but different colour or registration number) or just 'vroom-vroom' (any other motor vehicle). By the age of 7 he was interested in cars as many small boys are but could not identify an Avenger reliably. He could distinguish between some models and manufacturers by looking at shapes and name badges, but not the relatively unusual model he knew five years earlier.

Box 10.6 Learning example

might help to understand the problems of machine learning. The model has four elements:

world	something about which the machine has to acquire knowledge;
performance	some way of knowing how well it (the machine) is doing in some task in the world;
knowledge base	a store of rules, concepts, procedures, etc., which is used to produce performance;
learning process	a procedure which can compare performance in some task with the world and produce a new or revised entry in the knowledge base.

Learning becomes a process of repetition of these elements – but it is not that simple! The major problem revolves around examples and counter-examples.

'It's the exception that proves the rule' is a well known, if misunderstood, proverb. 'Prove' here is used in the sense of testing rather than verifying. Humans learn by constructing rules and proving them   testing the rules to see when they work and when they break down. For example, here is a proposed rule for deciding whether an object is a car.

> The object is large enough to contain at least one person, it has some transparent surfaces, a metal body, four wheels, makes a noise and propels itself mechanically when occupied by at least one person.

Box 10.7 Rules for learning

10.5.2 Expert systems vs machine learning

Davidson (1991) explains very clearly the differences between the expert systems approach and the machine learning approach. By quoting several examples, he highlights that machine learning 'is the reverse of an expert system. An expert system has to be given rules and it uses those rules. The (machine learning) program actually discovers the rules.' Very often users do not know what they do not know; they need to extract unknown information from large databases. This has been a problem of *information systems* for many years; since the 1960s management information systems have required managers to specify precisely the sort of information they need to do their jobs, sometimes years in advance of the programs to produce the information being written. Decision support tools such as spreadsheets were developed to meet the perceived need of managers in the early 1980s for software which allowed them to manipulate data without the need to employ analysts and programmers, thus saving costs and, more importantly, getting answers in hours/days instead of months/years.

Machine learning allows the computer to emulate a human statistician in looking for patterns in data; it is deviations from the norm which are significant and these are revealed in sequences of numbers. The expert system requires that the 'normal' values are defined so that unusual patterns may be found. But this presumes that the user knows and can define normal, an assumption which cannot be made. The learning computer has software rules for finding norms and deviations in any data, finding out *facts* which the user and the programmer did *not* know. Thus the machine learning approach is the next stage along the road from predetermined MIS via DSS to systems which will find patterns in the data for human investigation. Not all suggestions will be meaningful, but many will be. Box 10.8 gives some typical examples of applications of machine learning.

- Oil and gas exploration companies are using machine induction software to find unknown factors in geological data which might affect the returns on finds.
- Finance companies are using similar software to develop rules for money and stock market trading based on past data.
- A US computer manufacturer found that one operator was responsible for the majority of persistent faults on a disk drive. Investigation revealed that this was due to poor training.

Box 10.8 Machine learning applications

10.5.3 Problems in the learning process

There are several serious problems with simple models of learning. Overcoming these problems is the goal of machine learning research in many universities. This is likely to be done by improving the model of learning used by the computer (the software) and possibly by changing the type of computer which learns. The problems identified in machine learning are:

noise	irrelevant signals in the real world which require processing in order to ignore them;
vocabulary	the initial choice of the terms used to describe the world is particularly important as these determine the types of question the machine can ask about;
inheritance	the need to describe examples of objects in terms of more general objects from which a specific thing 'inherits' properties;
sub-optimisation	the tendency of machines to stop learning if any small change produces a 'worse' performance, even if a big change would produce 'better' performance;
changing world	as the machine learns new rules, the world may change or its understanding may lead to later rules conflicting with earlier rules.

Any software which is going to make machine learning a practical proposition for application in organisations on a larger scale than at present will have to address and solve these problems.

New computer architectures

Most computers work on the basis of a central processing unit which serially processes instructions held in memory – the *von Neumann* architecture after the first person to describe this type of computer. Improved performance is based on performing the same tasks more and more quickly through faster memory and CPU. However, another type of computer exists which works on a different principle, somewhat akin to the way the brain works. Known as a *neural net*, this computer manipulates data in a new way and holds many promises for the future. In particular, a neural net exhibits learning behaviour very similar to that shown by humans – it can be treated as an empty machine, as noted at the start of this section.

10.6 REVISION NOTES

1. Knowledge-based systems allow computers to manipulate facts about specific subject areas called domains.
2. A KBS consists of a knowledge base, an inference engine and a database.
3. A knowledge base stores production rules.

4.   An inference engine is software which can simulate reasoning by interpreting the rules in the knowledge base.

5.   Knowledge engineering is the process of eliciting and representing in a knowledge base the skills and expertise of humans.

6.   Inference uses the rules of logic to arrive at conclusions.

7.   Both deductive reasoning and inductive reasoning can be used in knowledge engineering to manipulate facts.

8.   An expert system is software which encapsulates the skills and experience of a human expert. It simulates the human reasoning process.

9.   Expert systems can be applied to many areas of human skill, whether intellecual or not.

10. Expert systems can be constructed by the use of software shells (generators) or special purpose programming languages.

11. Machine learning tries to avoid the problem of knowledge engineering by getting the system to learn rules, rather as a human child does.

12. There are six different types of learning process.

13. The business applications of machine learning are still limited, but new understanding and computers based on neural nets may improve the use of this technique.

10.7 SELF-TEST QUESTIONS

1.   Define the term 'production rule'.

2.   What is an inference engine?

3.   Why is knowledge elicitation difficult?

4.   Outline the differences between 'deductive' and 'inductive' reasoning.

5.   What is goal in knowledge engineering?

6.   Define the term 'expert system'.

7.   What is an expert system shell?

8.   Name two expert system languages.

9.   Explain the difference between a machine learning system and an expert system.

10. Outline some problems with the use of machine learning in a business environment.

10.8 FURTHER READING

1. *Intelligent Knowledge-based Systems: An introduction*, O'Shea *et al.* (eds), Harper & Row: London, 1987. Chapter 10 on machine learning is difficult but worth persevering with.
2. *Striking gold in them thar databases*, C. Davidson; in *Computer Guardian*, 17 Oct 91, Guardian Newspapers, London, 1991.

Index